CALLED

Called

CLASSEMINARS, INC.

Stories of Faithfully
Living Out God's Purpose

CLASSBooks

CLASSBOOKS
Albuquerque, NM

Copyright © CLASSBOOKS, 2018

ISBN 978-1727064902

Editor Linda Gilden
Cover Art by Amy Allen
Cover Design by Maddie Scott
Interior Art by Linda Goldfarb
Interior Design by kae Creative Solutions

Published in the United States of America.

All rights reserved. No part of this publication may be reproduced, stored in a retrieval system, or transmitted in any form or by any means -- electronic, mechanical, photocopy, recording, or any other -- except for brief quotations in printed reviews, without the prior permission of the publisher.

Scripture quotations marked (NIV) are taken from the Holy Bible, New International Version®, NIV®. Copyright © 1973, 1978, 1984, 2011 by Biblica, Inc.™ Used by permission of Zondervan. All rights reserved worldwide. www.zondervan.com The "NIV" and "New International Version" are trademarks registered in the United States Patent and Trademark Office by Biblica, Inc.™

Dedication

To the One who calls us all to

a life lived fully in His love.

TABLE OF CONTENTS

Introduction	9
A Family Call by Audrey V. Hailstock	11
Yes, Lord by Danni Andrew	15
Called for Such a Time by Michelle Denise Beal	19
A Purpose-full Journey by Brenda Blanchard	23
Called by Chante Coleman	27
Camp Claudine by TraciLynn	31
My Romans by Wendy T. Deluca	35
Called to Himself by Glenda Durano	39
We are Family by LuAnn Edwards	43
Daughter of the King! by Rebecca Frock	47
Listen for the Whistle by Linda Gilden	51
Called to Stay Put by Linda Goldfarb	53
The Call to Storytelling by Carolyn Braswell Greene	57
Fire in My Bones by Audrey V. Hailstock	61
Called to Serve by Lessie Harvey	65
You're Called to Write When…by Linda Jewell	69
Peace at Last by Carole Klock	73
God's Miracle Plan by Marilyn Neuber Larson	77
Change of Plans—Funeral Cancelled by Sharon Kern McCall	81
Give Me a Sign by Susan Parlato Revels	85
Sock Monkey Christmas by Dan Rosecrans	89

Are you THAT Person? By Laura Rosecrans	93
Called to Trust God by Mykaela Savage	97
Called to a Journey by Naomi Stahnke	101
Fly Like an Eagle by Diane Stelter	105
Dread Becomes Joy by Charlotte Wheat	109
Revelations on a Hiking Trail by Randy Windt	113
Called to Service by James Wininger	117
More Than Birds by Richelle Wright	121
Where are the Rest? by Joyce Zook	125
Called to Encourage by Lessie Harvey	129
Rough Wooden Boxes by Linda Jewell	133
He Has a Plan by Gerry Wakeland	137
Acknowledgments	141

Introduction

Called is one of those words with many meanings. For some of us, it means to have a conversation by phone. For others, vocal calling is a way to summon. The word called may bring to mind the name that was given to you by your earthly parents; they called you Mary or Blake, or Chris. For those who are believers, the word called may refer to God speaking in a specific way to your heart.

Even though we may define the word in many different ways, the stories in this book include the latter. Listening for the call of God is not always easy, but when we clearly hear His direction, it is a time for rejoicing.

Being called by God to be one of His children is the ultimate calling. His plan includes making us part of His family. Our hope is that everyone reading this book will already be part of God's family. But we also know that some of our readers have chosen to read this because a family member wrote a story. Or some were intrigued with the title or for another reason. Perhaps a few readers in that group have never felt the call of God.

For you, the message we hope you hear from this book is, "God loves you and He wants you to be part of His family." God wants that so much that He sent His Son to die for you. Don't let another day go by without confessing your sin and need to Him and asking Him to live in your heart. Then you will spend eternity with Him.

God's calling is precious and the foundation of a life filled with joy. *Called* illustrates that on every page. We are thankful we have stories to share, and that for every story in this book, there are so many more.

> "And we know that in all things God works
> for the good of those who love him, who have
> been called according to his purpose"
> (Romans 8:28 NIV).

A Family Call

Audrey V. Hailstock

As a child, getting lost on 297 acres of an amusement park was daunting to say the least. Our father was in charge of planning this trip and had planned it before school was out. The destination was Six Flags over Georgia, and we could hardly wait to get there. This particular return to the park was different because we were older and had grown enough to ride the bigger, faster rollercoasters, enjoy the entertainment, eat the footlongs, and try to win as many toys, playing those nearly-impossible-to-win games that looked so easy. We couldn't wait to venture out and experience the park like never before.

My brothers and I could not sleep the night before because of the excitement of the thrills and shrills that awaited us the following day. Morning finally came and not a moment too soon. We arrived at the park without too many, "Are we there yet?" inquires. Instructions were to 1.) follow closely, since we no longer had to hold hands, and 2.) don't get distracted. Needless to say, at the ages of eight and seven, my older brother and I got distracted and separated from our parents and younger brother. Though our wondering, whimsical eyes were off our parents and we were separated for a short period, our parents were watching. Distractions can be detrimental to us at any age, but especially when we are young and especially when we have a calling on our lives.

This is why in Matthew 16:24 (NIV) Jesus said to his disciples, "Whoever wants to be my disciples must deny themselves and take up their cross and follow me."

Disciples, deny, and follow are the key words related to a calling. We must be disciplined enough to not be easily distracted. We must deny the desire to do our will rather than the Father's. And we must strive to follow the directions our God gives us whether or not we agree with them, understand them, or feel adequate enough to handle them. The plan is that we arrive at the destination God has prepared for us.

God knows the plans He has for us – plans to give us a future and a hope. The weight of personally being called into the ministry can be heavy, but when you couple that with being married to someone who is also called, the adventure moves to another level. Because you are one, if one is called, one must go. That's not always easy. It can be downright demanding, intrusive, overwhelming, and uncertain…sort of like an amusement park at Halloween, when things are put in place to deliberately scare you and confuse you, causing you to get more tricks than treats. You don't know what to expect or what's around the next corner. You do know that the rollercoaster rides can take your breath or make you lose your stomach. But because it's God calling, you don't want to say no, or at least not for too long.

Instead, you want to hear God, respond with a yes, and then follow in obedience. Sarai and Abram set such an example when the Lord said to Abram, "Go forth from your country, and from your relatives and from your father's house, to the land which I will show you; and I will make you a great nation, and I will bless you and make your name great and so you shall be a blessing. And I will bless those who bless you and curse those who curse you" (Genesis 12:1-3 NAS). This is interesting to me because Sarai went along for the ride just like many pastors' wives must go along with the call, leave what is familiar and comfortable and follow wherever our heavenly Father leads.

When my husband was called to become the pastor of a church in a new city, it was not what I expected or wanted. It required that we move away from our parents, relatives, and friends and from the home we had just built two years prior. It was my husband's calling, but because we are one family, it was our calling. We had to deny ourselves, follow God's leading and stay focused on our calling.

God's blessings await you and countless others even when the mysteries of ministry call for you to deny yourself and follow Christ.

Father, teach me to always obey whatever you say and follow You wherever you lead. Amen.

Audrey V. Hailstock's passion is living the intensified life. She helps women move from marginal living to exceptional living. She is a powerful teacher, preacher, and praise and worship leader who loves letting her light shine.

Yes, Lord!

Danni Andrew

My mom's favorite Bible verse was "And we know that in all things God works for the good of those who love him, who have been called according to His purpose" (Romans 8:28 NIV). She quoted it all the time.

My mom passed away July 31, 2011. One month later to the day, on my birthday, I received an email telling me I was going to my first CLASS Writers Conference. I knew exactly how things would go. Soon I would marry the man of my dreams and I would be a best-selling author, traveling the world with my doting husband. I would be fifty pounds thinner, of course.

Here I am six years later, I have published my third book and I am traveling, speaking and well, I am not fifty pounds lighter. Let's say I am probably at least 200 pounds lighter. There is no Mr. Wonderful. There was one guy who nearly killed me in a Jeep rollover accident which ejected me and missed crushing me by three feet. I'm still not married and I'm actually fine with my marital status but the books have yet to hit the *New York Times* best seller list.

God doesn't promise us that we will get our every little whim according to our wishes. He promises that all things work for our good. I have seen the preachers who preach that if we want the new car it is ours, but I don't believe God is really in the new car business unless the new car is really what we need. He is in the need business not the want business.

When I walked into CLASS for the first time I was terrified. There was also an underlying excitement which could not be denied. I had no idea what I needed, but God knew. My apartment is not in the best part of town but it is one I can afford and fits my needs well. Two years ago my decision to move to Albuquerque was the realization of a long-held dream. I have no idea where this fabulous adventure is going to take me. But I do know, God has never left me hungry or begging for bread. I also know I am humbled at the opportunities that have been given me. God has taken such good care of me it is very rare that I question He will answer a prayer. I have published devotionals, travel articles, and now my own books which makes my heart swell with pride. I am a Distinguished Toastmaster with many hours on the stage and am about to embark on a journey that I have no idea where I am going. But God knows. This is the beauty of my journey. I feel like I am standing on the edge of a dream. My mom said this verse over and over so many times that it became imprinted on my brain and I didn't even think about what it meant until much later in life. My plans have become His plans and I am blessed beyond my wildest dreams. I am grateful for where I am and I am thankful for the peace of mind just knowing that no matter what happens I am going to be taken care of because the God of heaven cares enough about me to reach down and take care of me.

My life did not begin to turn around until I said a very simple prayer, it was "Yes Lord, do whatever You want!" It was a prayer of exhaustion, but I meant every word. I no longer cared what the outcome was. I had finally learned that beautiful truth that all things truly do work together for good because He loves me more than I love myself and He knows better than I do. Sometimes the best thing we can do for ourselves is to simply, give up. If you are struggling with a decision or worried about what life is going to bring to you next, just pray a simple prayer and give up.

Danni Andrew is a motivational speaker and teacher as well as an award-winning artist. She paints oil on canvas. Danni is a Distinguished Toastmaster and has published three books. Her latest book *Bipolar Disorder Doesn't Have to be Depressing* was released in September 2017. Danni lives in Albuquerque, New Mexico, with her dogs Bella and Boots.

CALLED FOR SUCH A TIME

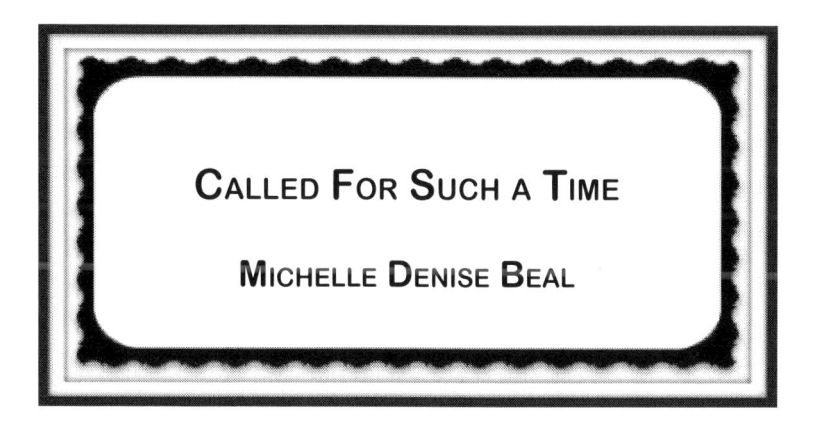

MICHELLE DENISE BEAL

We all are "called," set aside to serve, for a specific purpose in the kingdom of God. This was the case in the story of Queen Esther. God set her up for an assignment that wasn't just any kind of assignment. It was life changing and lifesaving; not just for her, but for all the of Jews. God had a divine plan to reveal His sovereignty and love for His people.

What's so interesting about her story is that God literally called her, before she even knew who she really was. Nothing about her life was normal. Technically she was an orphan, she had no mother or father (Esther 2:7), but was raised by her uncle, Mordecai. But the favor of God was richly upon her life. I can only imagine what her thinking must have been when it was proposed to her to help God's people. I'm sure her question was, "Who am I to be called for such an assignment?"

God gave her special favor with King Ahasuerus, as he was looking for a new queen to replace Queen Vashti.

Was it coincidence or divine purpose? Her story was more than the king needing a new queen. It was purpose! It was destiny! Simply put, it was a divine "call" upon her life.

What has God called you to do in this season? Is it possible God has been grooming you all of your life for a unique call and purpose? Are you feeling like Esther must have felt, by thinking of her obscure past? A past of the unknown? A past of a fragmented life. Are you thinking to yourself, who am I to change and help a generation of Gods people that are in trouble? We all can contest that our nation is in trouble. Do you feel and see the urgency demanded of your "call?" If you do, please take note of Esther's complete surrender and obedience to the "call." So much so, she replied with, "if I perish, I perish!" Esther's story resonates even in our time.

What have you been set aside and called to do at such a time as this? You and only you can give the answer. Hopefully your answer will be, "Here I am Lord, send me." God has set you aside for such as time as this. Be Nike, and "JUST DO IT"! God is patiently waiting on you.

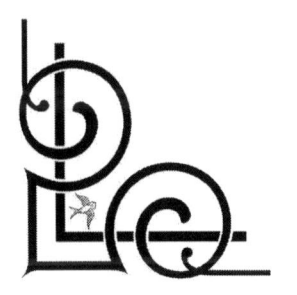

"Therefore, will the Lord wait, that he may be gracious unto you..."
(Isaiah 30:18).

*Lord Jesus, we thank you for reminding us of the "call"
that is on our lives. Help us to serve and surrender to all
that you have purposed in our hearts. In Jesus Name!
Amen!*

Michelle Denise Beal—mother, grandmother, pastor, author, and true worshipper. Loves God, His people, and has purposed in her heart to finish everything God has called her to do. Her deepest desire is to be a balanced woman and servant after God's own heart.

A Purpose-full Journey

Brenda Blanchard

As a child, I used to practice my penmanship often. If I made a mistake or the writing appeared less than perfect, I'd tear out the page from my Big Chief pad, wad it into a ball, and throw it into the trashcan. I absolutely loved the way writing something well made me feel.

Besides writing, I liked to talk and perform. When I was in the first or second grade, I informed my mom I was going to be a missionary and preach about Jesus. When we went camping as a family, I gathered the surrounding campers' kids on Sunday and pretend to be a preacher, telling them Jesus loved them. But, the enemy has a way of dashing dreams, and when my parents divorced in my early teens, I started doubting whether Jesus loved me and questioned if He was God. I began reading about other religions.

Since English and Theatre were my favorite two classes throughout my school days, I acquired both majors in college. At 18, I professed "Jesus is Lord" and began sharing the Gospel with others through Campus Crusade for Christ and one-on-one encounters. I took the calling of all Christians to share Jesus seriously and even became the Chaplain in my Tri-Sigma Sorority house.

Upon college graduation, I married my high school and college beau. Although I knew we were unequally yoked, I disobeyed the Lord and married him anyway. I started out as a high school teacher, but ended up as a General Manager for hotels. Due to his work, we moved over 17 times in our 10 years of marriage which simply made a teaching career difficult. During these years, we attended church, but my enthusiasm for sharing Christ diminished. I also started writing several books, but never finished any of them.

After our divorce, I felt confused, abandoned, and weak-minded. I knew I needed to rely on Jesus, but I kept looking for a man to give me only what Jesus could fill within me. Instead of going to the Source, I went to a source who appeared godly, and I ended up getting hurt emotionally, physically, and spiritually.

Following this traumatic experience, the Lord kept talking to me about writing a book. However, I didn't want to write the book He required of me. I kept trying to start other books, and He'd let me get a couple of chapters written, but then He'd stop me. My mind would only reflect on the story He wanted me to tell. I kept ignoring Him until I ended up flat on my back in a bed.

In 1998, a neurologist diagnosed me with Multiple Sclerosis, and I used a wheelchair to move about. I began the novel, *Angel of Light*, while I lay in bed.

Amid these circumstances, the Lord reminded me He never leaves me, and He always loves me. The Lord touched me and within six months of His divine embrace and words to my spirit, I moved from the wheelchair to a walker, then to a four-pronged cane to a cane to walking on my own. Two different neurologists had given me three to five years before I would be unable to do anything for myself. Now, I'm feeling led to put the novel out to others. During these years of writing, editing, and rewriting, He called me to pen and lead a monthly in-home Bible study to strengthen and disciple other women. Sisters in Christ Bible Study has been meeting for almost 19 years. He also called me to write various short stories, articles, devotions which have been published in many venues of print. In addition, He called me to speak at retreats, ladies' groups, and writing groups. For almost 15 years, I've been called to lead the Christian Writers Group of Greater San Antonio to encourage and assist others in the writing and editing of works for His glory. And, He gave me a truly godly man to call my husband.

I have learned God's calling may not be an easy one, but His calling brings about His desired fruit. I praise Him for choosing me to be a bearer of His Light. For I do know, "…God causes all things to work together for good to those who love God, to those who are called according to His purpose" (Romans 8:28 NASB).

Father, help me be obedient. Make me holy. Amen.

Brenda Blanchard is a speaker and writer with bylines in magazines, compilation books, and newspapers. She's Co-President for Christian Writers Group and founded The Door of Hope Ministries and Sisters in Christ Bible Studies. See www.brendablanchard.com

CALLED

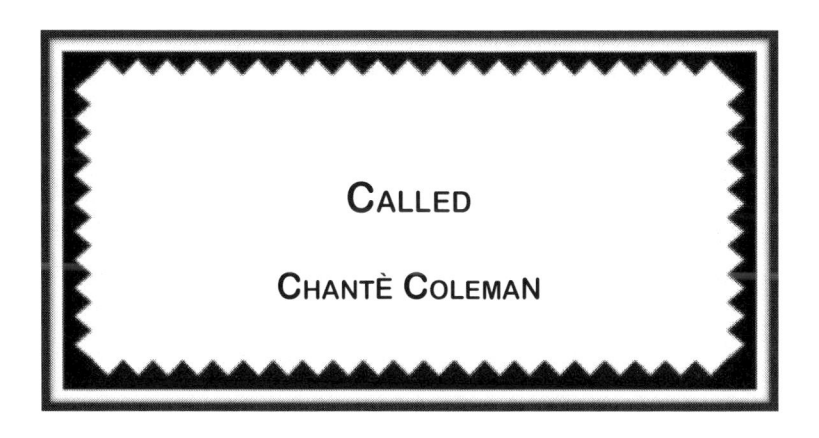

CHANTÈ COLEMAN

I was called by my momma to clean my room, pray, and make good grades. Daddy called me to play softball, practice basketball, and be kind. Out on the farm, I was called to plow, plant, and water my grandma's cornstalk. Oh yes, I've been called to many things throughout spring, summer, fall, and winter. I was called a military brat in Germany and Belgium. A student at Maryland University, Troy State, and University of New Mexico. The best gift of my life calls me mommy, which causes me to smile, cry, and at times be frustrated. Chief Master Sergeant Shelf calls me an Airman. And to most of my friends in the Federal world I'm called an investigator. On the movie set, I'm called the producer, director, and writer. The world calls me to many roles, but one day God called me to be His own.

God's been calling me my whole life. He tried to get through to my heart, but the line would be busy, or sent to voicemail, and sometimes He'd get hold of me but the reception was bad because of the season in my life. When I finally picked up and cleared the airwaves, God revealed He had called me to Himself before He had woven me in my momma's stomach. He'd called my momma and my daddy to marry, have a child, and raise it up in relationship with Him.

I was called to pray by my momma. I was called to be kind by my daddy. I was called to spread the gospel by my grandma. I was called to be trained up by the universities. I was called to be obedient by the military. I was called to carry life by my child. I was called to help those in need and poor in spirit with each case I was given. Throughout all these callings, God was calling me to Himself. He was and is still refining me to be His pen. A willing heart that would express how Jesus Christ, His Son, saved us. How God loves us. And how the Helper, the Holy Spirit resides in us. The best call of my life was from Jesus Christ who calls me His child, His friend, His special treasure, and His very own. What a wonderful eternal gift to be called by God. He's calling, will you pick up?

Father, I pray that my sister or brother in Christ who is reading this seeks Your will for their life. I pray they have a clearer understanding of Your infinite love. You are a

Father who cares for His children. Everything we go through whether it is good or bad, the challenge is drawing us closer to You.

I pray they would answer Your call today. In Jesus name, Amen!

Chantè Coleman—Servant of God, daughter, granddaughter, mother, friend, USAF Airman, federal investigator, college graduate, writer, filmmaker, singer

CAMP CLAUDINE

TraciLynn

I know God has called me and He's calling you too. He tells us in Isaiah 61, His Spirit is upon us and He has equipped us.

As the single mother of two small boys, I didn't get to spend as much time with them as I would have liked. Working two jobs and going to school in between left us little time to play but when we did, we played hard.

As the seasons passed my boys grew into men, and oh how the grandchildren have multiplied. I love my boys deeply and it amazes me how God has ignited that love to include other children, my grandchildren, neighborhood children, church children—all children.

The first time God revealed His hand of love was during a sleepover with my grandchildren. The giggles from my grandkids as we pulled the mattresses off the beds and put them on the floor under the tents we made was a true sign. God touched my heart and I recognized it was Him. The tents were wonderful for snuggling while we watched movies eating popcorn and ice cream. And yes, at the same time, it's Grammie's house.

Before long it was campouts in the backyard inviting the neighbor kids and church kids. Lots of hugs, laughter, and letting them know how much God loves them. We had dance offs and flashlight hide and seek. By this time, building the campfire and hunting for sticks to make S'mores had become a solid tradition. There were also boo boos to bandage, noses to wipe, and feelings to negotiate. I've learned, little girls can be very hard on each other leaving holes of opportunities for sharing Jesus and God's love.

This year I moved to a new home so I wasn't going to have the campout. I believed it wouldn't be a big deal—and then I went bowling with several of the kids. They started in with "when is the next campout, what are we doing this time?" I started to explain I was in a new home and still had boxes everywhere. Did that deter them? No! They're kids. Who cares about unpacked boxes when there is fun to be had and memories to be made. That's when I felt the Lord tug on my heart. He is the author of the campouts. And so it was on!

Lots of planning to be done. My new corner-lot home has a smaller back yard with lots of front and side room. Every year the kids multiply, this year there were 26! They ranged in age from 1 to 17 years old. Therefore, I borrowed another large tent and enlisted the help of some family and friends. As a result, Camp Claudine was born. We made tie-dyed t-shirts with sharpies and rubbing alcohol, had water balloon fights, lots of grilling, lessons on first aid, sidewalk chalk drawings, a dance off, topping it off with a guitar and amplifier for some live singing and worship. All of this took place under two huge trees, one in the front yard and one in the back between the two large strategically placed tents. Both trees had two swings each. You wouldn't think a swing could bring so much joy—it was non stop.

On Saturday evening we split the kids into two groups and watched with joy as they made sock puppets, the bigs helping the littles without even being asked. They had hot glue guns, feathers, buttons, pipe cleaners, yarn, glitter, and more, everything I had in my craft closet, and the key ingredient was imagination. As they worked on their creations each team had to come up with a skit to perform. We created a backdrop to perform behind, with lights pointing at them and waited for night. We were truly entertained and laughed so hard our sides were hurting.

Sunday morning, Jesus First, overflowed with worshipping children in a sea of colorful Camp Claudine T-shirts. God touched so many lives, more then I could have imagined when He called me to suffer the children.

When God asks you to do something, He equips you. My calling is anchored in Mark 9:37 NKJV, "Whoever receives one of these little children in My name receives Me; and whoever receives Me, receives not Me but Him who sent Me."

Lord, help others to know their true calling anchored in Your Word. Amen.

TraciLynn is a mother, Grammie, worshiper, prayer warrior, church elder, writer, painter, cosmetologist and master barber. CampClaudine@gmail.com

My Romans

Wendy T. DeLuca

The display at a local Christian bookstore caught my attention. The words "Birth Verse" emblazoned the top. I'd never heard that term before. I stepped closer and read how each Birth Verse correlates a chapter and verse of the Bible with the month and day a person was born.

I searched until I found my birth date, 8/30. The scripture was Romans 8:30 (NLT): "And having chosen them, he called them to come to him. And having called them, he gave them right standing with himself. And having given them right standing, he gave them his glory."

My verse. The story of how the Lord changed my life in three short sentences.

Romans was one of the first books I read in the Bible. This was a good starting point because Paul's words helped give a foundation for my new faith. I have now read Romans nine times, so my birth verse has become more meaningful to me.

I was amazed that the creator of the universe chose me, even before I chose His Son. His love made me feel special. Like I mattered. I haven't always been wanted. My earthly father left when I was a baby. I didn't always feel accepted by my peers. This led to insecurity.

When my eyes were opened to how much the Lord loved me, I started to follow Him. My whole life was transformed.

God had a plan and purpose for my life beyond my wildest dreams, but to carry it out I had to come to know Him first. I had to feel loved and secure in that love before I could go out and do His work. God called us to Him but also called us to do something for Him.

I understood God loved me and forgave me, but it was hard to comprehend that He would use me. I lived my life far away from Him and hurt myself and others with my harmful, self-destructive behavior. The result was broken relationships, health problems, and financial struggles.

God used pain to draw me closer to Him. My struggles tested me, helped me grow stronger, and prepared me for what was ahead. The Lord wants me to share my experiences with others who are hurting. To comfort others with the comfort He has given me. This is my calling. I am an encourager—both in my personal life and in my job as a professional counselor. But I must be vulnerable and honest. Admit I don't have everything worked out in my life. But through Jesus I am made right with God. Living out my purpose is a daily struggle. Sometimes I feel as though I let God down. I still battle selfishness and impatience. My tendency toward perfectionism causes stress and anxiety. Not only for myself, but for others as well. When I am away from work, I don't always practice what I teach my clients. I often allow busyness to distract me from more important things. Like my relationship with the Lord. I beat myself up when I don't live up to my own standards.

I am not alone in this battle. All have sinned and fallen short of the glory of God. But the Lord reminds me to give myself grace, just as He does.

When I am made right with God, He gives me His glory. What does that mean? How do know I have it? I show God's glory when I:

- Choose joy, praise Him, and give thanks in spite of my trials.

- Don't take offense or keep a record of wrongs. Instead I love and pray for my enemies and those who have hurt me.

- See that God is working in my situation even when I don't feel Him. I may not understand the pain I am going through, but I trust Him even when I am discouraged and start to lose hope.

- Look beyond outward appearance and behavior and see a person the way God created them. I realize they are blinded to the truth and don't understand what they are doing. They are lost.

God's glory shines through my story. I walked away from the Birth Verse display with greater understanding of who God created me to be. I am: Chosen. Called. Justified. Glorified.

What experiences in your life can God use to show His glory to others?

Lord, help me to trust Your plan for my life. I may not always understand it, but I know You will use everything together for my good and for Your glory. Amen.

To find out your Birth Verse, visit http://www.storkie.com/birthverse.aspx

Wendy T. Deluca, a U.S. Navy Veteran and Clinical Therapist, provides faith-based counseling. A graduate of Liberty University and Australia's Hillsong International Leadership College, she writes to encourage single women to find contentment and joy. WendyDeluca.com

CALLED TO HIMSELF

GLENDA DURANO

What would happen, if, instead of seeking God's will for the future, we focused on seeking God right now?

For six months, I'd been searching for my mid-life purpose. I'd pleaded with God for direction, spoken to multiple career counselors, and done everything that the books said I needed to do in order to discover my late-in-life calling.

Still, I had nothing. But I knew it was out there. After all, Jeremiah 29:11 NIV promises, "For I know the plans I have for you... plans to give you hope and a future." Would God's Word prove itself true for a middle-aged mom just as it had proved true for my daughter months earlier?

Like many high school seniors, my daughter Amberle had fretted over her college search, desperately wanting God to show her exactly where He wanted her to go. One day, after months and mounds of university applications, Amberle announced, "I know exactly what God wants me to do about college." I assumed she'd had an epiphany and heard a voice from heaven, until she said, "All I have to do is follow God. Right now." Before she could pursue God's plan, Amberle realized she first had to pursue His Person. Ultimately, she heard His plan as well.

After twenty-one years of being a homeschool mom, I needed to do the same thing. My nest and my schoolroom were empty, and I was ready to step back into the workplace, discover what God had for me, and make a difference in the world.

As I pondered my future, fear overwhelmed me. What if I failed? What if I no longer had what it takes? What if I couldn't find a job? Regrets over my former mistakes and fears of my unknown future strangled my self-confidence. I had to stop thinking about the "what if" and focus on the "Who is."

In John 8:58, Jesus refers to Himself as "I am." Unfortunately, however, believers often look for God and His will somewhere in the distant future—not in the here and now. God equips each of us for His particular purposes, but it is a process, and every moment is a piece of the puzzle. Hebrews 13:5 instructs, "Today, if you hear His voice…" Indeed, God is the God of the past and the God of the future, but it might serve us better to simply think of Him as the God of right now. As we seek Him— not just His will—He reveals His calling to us, and ultimately,

He is faithful to "fulfill His good purpose" (Philippians 2:13) in us.

Instead of searching for a calling that is future action-oriented—based purely on what we will do someday—how about searching for a calling that is relationally driven right now? A calling that focuses on who we are in Him, not just on what we do—one that means, as my daughter discovered, to "follow God. Right now."

Lord, as I pursue You, show me more of Yourself. I surrender myself to You and thank You for completing Your perfect will in my life. Amen.

Glenda Durano enjoys fulfilling multiple roles every day: homemaker, business owner, consultant, speaker, writer. Her ultimate desire, however, is not to be known for what she does, but rather, who she is: a child of God.

We are Family

LuAnn Edwards

At a time when I am hearing about the many problems with adoption and how detrimental it is to separate babies from their birth mothers, I still believe I was called by God to adopt. Despite the trauma this causes the child on into adulthood, it is not always possible for the birth mom to care for her child.

The adoptive parent's love, in combination with Christ's love, forms a family bond which will hopefully grow stronger over time. However, the trauma of being torn away from his mother is devastating for a child even though he may have been an infant at the time. This may cause issues with a lack of trust toward, or attachment to, his new parents. The child may subconsciously fear his new parents may also abandon him, or he may grow up with the belief something is wrong with him and that is why his mother left him. Although we have experienced attachment and abandonment issues in our home, I still believe God placed the desire to adopt in my heart.

The adoption road should not be traveled by the faint-hearted. There are dramatic situations to be faced throughout the years when attachment and/or abandonment issues surface. Yet children need a home, someone to meet their needs, someone to love them, someone to help them through the rough times, and someone to share Christ's love.

While praying and seeking the Lord for wisdom before our adoption, I read about children in Third World countries fending for themselves in area dumps looking for food to survive, children living on the streets at age eight, and girls being sold into prostitution at age five. These stories and knowing there were so many children needing homes disturbed me. My heart was filled with compassion for them.

At the time, we had a child in college and a senior in high school. As I prayed and fasted asking the Lord what He wanted us to do, I felt His direction to adopt a Third World country child and provide a Christian home for her. Since we had two older children who would be moving out soon, I wanted to be sure this was God's calling.

One of the verses the Lord gave me to lean on was Isaiah 58:11, "The Lord will guide you continually, and satisfy your soul in drought, and strengthen your bones; you shall be like a watered garden, and like a spring of water, whose waters do not fail" (NKJV) The Lord guides, strengthens, and satisfies me in times of weariness. He pours out His blessings upon me—refreshing me and supplying my needs. The struggles have sometimes been great, but our God is greater. We have loved our daughter in the good times and loved her in the difficult times.

Would we do it again knowing what we know now? Knowing there could be difficulties with attachment? Knowing about the devastating pain and sorrow she most likely would experience due to the trauma of losing her biological family? A big resounding yes. How could we not? She is our daughter and we love her dearly. We are in this together. We are family.

Lord, I am thankful for Your blessings each day and for Your amazing grace. When times are tough, Your grace is with me. I find my strength and sufficiency in You.
Amen.

LuAnn Edwards and her husband Kenn live in Albuquerque, New Mexico. They have two adult children, a teenaged daughter, and three grandchildren. She enjoys reading, writing, hiking, and spending time with her family.

Daughter of the King

Rebecca Frock

I was the girl with seizures. The headaches and injuries to my body were a constant result of the violent thrashing started by an electrical brain storm. This convulsing kept me home from school often. My parents both worked, and I became a latch key kid. As I sat at home alone, mental flight was my treasured gift. In thought, I could fly high above my life and leave the mundane at behind. Not much made sense in between my seizure and recovery phases. I longed for more. I didn't know God then, but He knew me. My mom will tell you they didn't expect much from me. My epilepsy plagued every aspect of learning so what was the point in dreaming? My family valued education above all things and I failed. Remarkably, I graduated high school and managed to get into college. I was soaring again but this time there was no wind. I still didn't know God, yet He tended to me every day.

To say that I had to play catch up in college doesn't come close to explaining my learning curve. I had failed algebra in high school and now I found myself sitting in Advanced Experimental and Statistical Methods. I was flying again but now I wasn't in high school anymore. I was breaking every ill spoken word intended to ground me as I was lifted to heights that weren't meant for me. After all, I was the girl with seizures. Navigating my new-found freedom on campus with occasional emergency room visits became rich soil for growth. I began to sense a purpose for my life that was too big for me to understand.

Counseling and psychology fascinated me. Helping people and volunteering was invigorating. Theories of Personality and Abnormal Psychology became intriguing topics, yet I was a horrible test taker. My struggle with memory and concentration while dodging seizures and side effects was real. I used to say to myself, if only I could have a different brain. I still remember the shock of my family that "Becca got her degree!" After all, I was the girl with seizures. Through this affliction, however, I developed a bold, fearless approach to life. I knew each day could be my last. I could die at any moment with the lethal timing of seizures and circumstances that would cause my death. In fierce faith, I flew again, this time to New Mexico. I followed my heart.

Some in my family were outraged with "what ifs." How could I stay in New Mexico when no one in my family lived here to respond if I had a seizure? I wish I could say I prayed about it, but I still didn't know God. There was no prayer, only another flight plan. Working as a waitress while getting my master's degree in counseling was my new life. I'd bike or walk to and from school and work. On occasion, I'd wake up on the sidewalk, disoriented, and confused with a massive headache and a new set of injuries. God covered me in His protection and love before I even acknowledged His existence. Now, I was no longer the girl with seizures, I was becoming a woman with a dream. No amount of seizures was going to stop me from my dream. I was going to be a therapist. I was going to help hurting people.

Tragically, once I became a therapist I discovered that my dream job did not fulfill me. Disillusioned, I felt like a fraud. Daily, I was faced with the daunting task of giving people answers and hope that I didn't have. They didn't just want a Band-Aid for their suffering, they wanted restoration and transformation. My tool box didn't have these things. No amount of cognitive behavioral therapy imparted peace and joy. I came to the end of myself, disgusted with the lies I had pursued. Then I heard the truth. His name is Jesus. He lifted me so I could soar even before I knew Him. He gave me flight and called me His and now He was mine.

The Divine Counselor showed me how to counsel. He revived my love for helping the hurting by resurrecting my career into the calling He had always intended it to be. I invite Him into every one of my sessions and I watch Him heal His flock every day. It's no longer my practice, it's His. Now, He allows me to observe His transformational work in every heart He sends me. He whispers, "love them as I love you.." Just when I thought I couldn't soar any higher,

He asked me to cast my net even wider and share His message beyond my office walls. He asked me to write and counsel. As a daughter of the King I will obey and honor His plans for my life. It is no longer I who live but Christ who lives in me. (Galatians 2:20) Walking in your calling requires ridding yourself of labels and titles designed by humanity. He is calling you Beloved, rise and soar!

For two decades Rebecca Frock MA, LPCC has counseled New Mexicans through tough times. Her specialty is Christ-centered professional counseling for anxiety, depression, and trauma. Her blog will help you find hope and encouragement. Morethanablogger.com Rebeccafrock.net, @FrockRebecca

LISTEN FOR THE WHISTLE

LINDA GILDEN

Growing up in a neighborhood full of children made for many long afternoons and evenings of play. We played ball, listened for the train so we could run to the bridge and feel it shake as the train passed by, and created an entire subdivision in the "Little Woods" so we could practice being grown up! During those fun play dates there was one thing that never changed—my siblings and I knew our time was up when we heard Dad's whistle.

My dad had a whistle that could be heard several blocks away. It was distinct. Though there were multiple species of birds in the neighborhood, when Dad whistled there was no mistake that it was time to come home. And no excuse was strong enough for us to ignore the whistle (unless we wanted to suffer the consequences later!).

Daddy's call was easily discerned from all other sounds. He was calling us to come home and we listened. Our obedience was of the utmost importance.

Now that I am older, Daddy doesn't have to use his whistle as much. But I am often reminded of the days of being ready to respond to his call.

Being obedient to the call of my earthly father was important during my early years and continues to be important as I want to benefit from his wisdom. But even more important is listening to God's "whistle." Many times I have felt the same sense of urgency when I realize He is speaking to me as I did when I heard my dad's whistle. The difference is that there are times when I don't respond to God's call as quickly as I should. I find a reason to procrastinate, it doesn't seem convenient, or I just pretend I didn't hear Him. Whatever the reason, I regret I'm not always a good listener.

God's call may not be a whistle. He speaks to each of us in different ways. But for me I want to listen. I want to hear his call and eagerly respond. When God calls, I want to run to Him with the same urgency and commitment I jumped on my bike and pedaled home when I heard my daddy's whistle. He told us, "My sheep listen to my voice; I know them, and they follow me" (John 10:27 NIV).

How about you? Are you listening?

Linda Gilden is an award-winning author, speaker, editor, ghostwriter, writing coach, personality consultant. Author of sixteen books and over a thousand magazine articles, Linda loves helping others discover the joy of writing. Linda loves every minute spent with her six grandchildren (great writing material!). Visit www.lindagilden.com.

Called To Stay Put

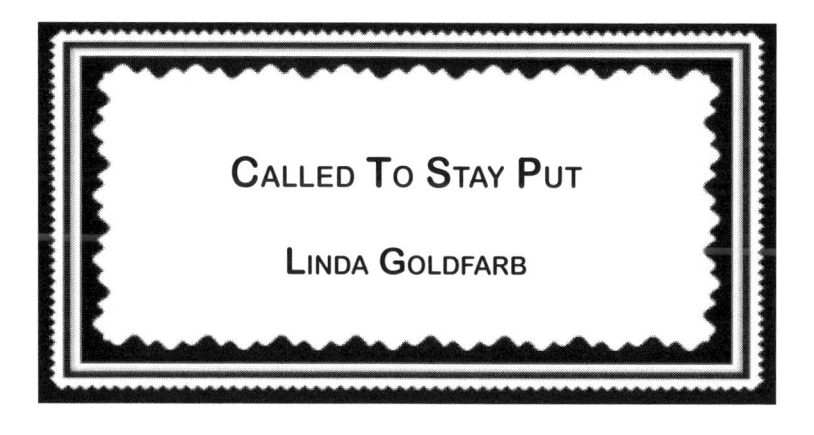

Linda Goldfarb

Silence resonated throughout the dining room, as eight of my dearest friends stared in my direction with a look of uncomfortable anticipation.

"God's will, God's way, and God's timing. That's all we're to pray for." I took another deep breath and waited for the air to settle. "Let's pray."

This not-so-routine routine always followed my travel debriefs. It's grown to be one of my most anticipated moments with the Live Powerfully Now board members and prayer warriors, after returning home from a ministry-based road trip.

We have a process. Meet at Carol's house, eat a light meal then gather together as I share my red-bench-moments (those, you-never-saw-it-coming, could-only-be-God moments) with the team.

Over the course of the next six years, God's will, God's way, and God's timing opened some unexpected doors while closing the ones my team would have chosen to be God's best.

Stepping away from a few prominent national and international platforms did not seem like forward-motion to my team or for that respect, people outside of my team. We prayed, and God closed doors.

The Lord says in Revelation 3:8, "Keep in mind, I know your deeds. See, I have placed before you an open door that no one can shut. I know that you have little strength, yet you have kept my word and have not denied my name." And what He says, He will hold true for those who love Him today. Therefore, I never seek a key to open a closed door, and as best as I can, I walk through the open ones with little hesitation.

His open doors have proven to be God's exact best for my ministry, my marriage, and my life. Staying put in my community forced me to narrow my ministry focus. Though I had a successful speaking and professional acting career, where I presented to a vast array of audiences nationally and internationally, my streamlined passion narrowed to influencing local parents with the truth on a weekly basis. What a change —right?

Holding an Advanced Diploma in Christian Life Coaching and an Advanced Certification as a Personalities instructor, I consider it an honor to personally help hundreds of parents grow from living a good life to experiencing God's best for their families each year. Specializing in relational communication has expanded my reach into local family-focused organizations such as the San Antonio Children's Protective Agency. My narrowed focus also allows me to help local struggling parents gain back custody of their children through my Parenting Awesome Kid's group coaching.

Staying put expanded my ministry to include my husband, Sam. Together, we work with local parents of junior golfers. We write for the Junior Golf Magazine and host bi-monthly seminars with our partners at The First Tee of Greater San Antonio.

Most assuredly, God's call on my life to stay put has grown me in relational ways I never would have experienced.

Are you struggling to experience God's calling; however, you're determined to have it your way? Might I suggest you take the next thirty days and just pray, "God's will, God's way, and God's timing, that's all I'm praying for." Then be willing and patient to walk through the doors He opens and turn away from those He closes. No searching for keys, no haggling, no compromising. You, too, may find staying put to be your highest calling, second only to sharing the good news of Jesus Christ with every breath you take.

Father God, thank You for opening and closing doors that no man can influence. Help us to see Your will and to wait on Your timing for the calling You have on our lives. As Your children, we desire to give You glory in and through our everyday actions. Help us, O Lord, to stay faithful to Your way. Amen.

Linda Goldfarb is widely recognized as a bold, passionate, and transparent communicator to parents and women. She influences lives, impacts families, and ignites hope through her writing, speaking, and coaching.
www.LivePowerfullyNow.org

THE CALL TO STORYTELLING

CAROLYN BRASWELL GREENE

"Tell a parable [story]…" (Ezekiel 17: 2 AMP)

Since the beginning of time believers have been called to communicate God's message to hostile audiences. When the prophet Ezekiel was charged with addressing the needs of wounded and traumatized exiles, he was instructed to tell a story. Stories get past our defenses. C. S. Lewis told fairytales and stories because they enabled him to convey biblical truth in a way that navigated past "watchful dragons," the gatekeepers of the human heart. Eugene Peterson author of *The Message* points out that "Jesus used stories to circle around his listener's defenses."

The stories Ezekiel wrote did just that, they stole past "watchful dragons," "circled reader's defenses" and seeped into human hearts. His stories help shaped the nation of Israel. They gave meaning to their experience of exile, provided direction for living, and enabled them to survive captivity.

Stories also play a major role in shaping American culture. In her book, *Uncle Tom's Cabin*, Harriet Beecher Stowe addressed the hardened hearts of white slave owners who viewed blacks as sub-human. She crafted a story she hoped would spread "the great Christian principle of brotherhood" and "good will" to white and black alike. Although Stowe's work is romantic and a bit melodramatic, the death of Uncle Tom at the hands of Simon Legree forced white readers to identify with Tom, a black man who faced trials with dignity and died victoriously. Stowe's story fueled the abolitionist movement and helped ignite the Civil War. Lincoln biographer, Herbert Donald, records that Lincoln greeted Harriet Stowe as, "the little lady who made this big war." Published in 1852, *Uncle Tom's Cabin* was the best-selling book of the 19th century, second only to the *Bible*. Stowe's book proved to be a rallying point that shaped American history and changed the lives of countless individuals.

Unfortunately, most Americans today are shaped by stories that come from Hollywood. Stories like *Star Wars* have had an immense effect on our culture. This iconic film was released during a dark time when American heroes and role models had been decimated by the Vietnam War and Watergate. The movie provided new heroes, enabled Americans to see themselves in a new light, and created hope for the future. Ezekiel, Stowe, and Lucas proved that story-tellers can be world changers.

As Shelley, a romantic poet, wrote, "Poets (and I would add storytellers) are the unacknowledged legislators of the world." The world desperately needs modern day Ezekiels and Stowes who can tell strong stories. Stories capable of making sense out of our lives, of shaping our faith, and providing hope for the future.

God is calling storytellers today to follow Ezekiel's example and tell a story, to mine the fertile stories of the Word and re-conceptualize them so that we too might address today's challenges and claim a future for our people.

What stories are we telling? The stories we tell may or may not chart the course of nations as those of Ezekiel and Stowe, but we can tell stories that transform lives and change the world one reader at a time.

Lord, thank-you for the powerful stories and marvelous characters that have shaped my life and my world. Help me answer the call to tell stories that make a difference and transform lives. Amen.

Carolyn Braswell Greene holds a MDIV from SWBTS and is a doctoral candidate at Ashland Theological Seminary. Carolyn is a pastor, speaker, formational counselor, and an inspiring storyteller. www.carolyngreene.me

Fire in My Bones

Audrey V. Hailstock

"She's dynamite! She's a fireball! She's the fussing preacher! She's Rev. Bunion Maker! I've heard it all." The most telling was when a lady said to me after I preached at her church, "Okay, I just want to thank you for slapping me up side my head, stepping on my corns, and bouncing me off the pews, okay…all right. And thank you so much because I needed it." Giving people what they need is my calling—the thing I was born to do. There is no doubt in my mind that God called me to preach His holy Word.

For many, "the call" is inexplicable. But for me, it was as simple as a thought God initially chose to place in my mind and subsequently speak out of my soul. This call was conceived so deeply within my soul that I felt it. I felt it before there was evidence of it. I felt it much like a woman with child feels and knows physically something is different long before others can see the evidence of the seed being carried. The spiritual signs can be mistaken for something else or even ignored out of fear, procrastination, or denial.

However, a true unction from God becomes increasingly clear and gets louder and louder within. Others may not have heard God calling me, but I sure did.

I knew there was something different within me when I said to my father what I felt deep within. One evening after listening to my father preach a fiery sermon, I recall vividly saying to him that I could hoop just like he hooped. Hooping is the excited, animated, climax of the sermon. I then mocked what my dad did at the end of his sermons, asking, "Can I get a witness?" Dad and Mom thought this was funny because I was only seven years old, but my spiritual development became more evident. While other young people were playing or partying, I was inside studying the Word of God with my mom, who was a strong Christian woman. We sat around the dining room table and studied the Sunday school lesson. I was drawn to Bible study and prayer meeting. I accepted Jesus as my Savior, was baptized, and grew closer to God. By the age of thirteen, I was teaching Sunday school and vacation Bible school. At fifteen, I was the secretary of Sunday school and on two choirs.

As a student at Erskine College, I confidently stated that I was called to be a world renown author and speaker. Even though I said it boldly, I questioned my qualifications and said I would speak passionately about things I truly believed in. As I grew in the knowledge of what God would have me do, I began reading through the Bible each year. Though my occupation was teaching, my vocation was preaching the Word of God and winning souls. I preached with such fervor that people said I was bootlegging the gospel because I had not preached the trial sermon to get a license. Little did they know that my husband, who is a pastor, would not allow me to preach because he did not agree with women being preachers. Talk about being between a rock and a hard place: the rock was Jesus and the hard place was not being allowed to do what I knew I was called to do. However, my mom had gone through the same thing with her calling until my father allowed her to do her trial sermon. Mom's patience paved the way for me.

God knew me before He formed me in my mother's womb, and before I came forth out of her womb, He sanctified me. And, like Jeremiah, God ordained me a prophet unto the nations. You see, along with the joys of my calling, I had to recognize and accept the realities of my calling. It was years later after sharing with my husband that I was called to preach, that I was allowed to go into the ministry.

Calling isn't private. It's personal. As God called Samuel, David, Ruth, and Mary the mother of Jesus, God is still pouring His Spirit on men and women to prophesy, according to Acts 2:18. I am humbled to serve God as I feed and love His sheep. The message of forgiveness is what kindles the fire within me to preach His Word.

Audrey V. Hailstock's passion is living the intensified life. She helps women move from marginal living to exceptional living. She is a powerful teacher, preacher, and praise and worship leader who loves letting her light shine.

CALLED TO SERVE

LESSIE HARVEY

I love telling others about Jesus Christ and how He is changing me, but for some reason, others are not always interested in hearing what I have to say. Maybe I am too passionate in my presentation or too preachy in trying to get my point across. But I really don't think those are the reasons. I've learned people are open to hearing and receiving what I have to say when they feel I am genuinely concerned about them. When I make a personal connection with people, listen to them, love them, and choose to walk beside them, then I am loving and serving Jesus because I am loving and serving others.

Initially, I couldn't understand why people were more concerned about themselves than Jesus until I remembered that I felt the same way before I accepted Jesus Christ as my Lord and Savior. Until then, I was not interested in hearing about Jesus—especially if I felt that the person telling me about Him acted as though I was invisible every other time they saw me. If Jesus was so great and so good, why didn't He help me through difficult situations, clear road blocks in my path, or surround me with people who truly cared for me? I didn't want any part of a God who played favorites.

Unlike me, Jesus knew who He was and why He was on earth. I did not know who I was or why I was born until I responded to God's call to me.

God's call was soft and gentle, not in my face or preachy. He was there when I needed someone to listen, to give hope, to comfort, and to encourage. When I read the Bible, I saw how He related to people. He was there for them and freely served them when they should have been serving Him. Imagine God, in the flesh, serving those He created rather than them serving Him. If Jesus could serve others, I wanted to be like Him. Therefore, I wanted to serve others too.

After I made the commitment to serve others, Jesus gave me many opportunities to serve. He sent people to spark my interest in attending a Bible college to discover who He is, to attend Bible Study Fellowship International to learn about Him, and to become part of CLASSeminars to prepare me to speak and write His words. Some of the people I met along the way, I could serve joyfully. Others, well let's just say God was doing a great work in me to bring me to the point of genuinely loving and serving them. Has God brought you to the point of serving others? Are you ready to accept this challenge? If so, know that serving others changes you from the inside because God is transforming you to become more like Him. Enjoy serving!

> *Father, thank You for giving me the opportunity to become more like You. Please give me a heart and desire to serve others so they may experience Your goodness and loving kindness on earth. Amen.*

Lessie Harvey lives in Maryland with her husband, Jesse. Her three adult children and grandchildren are near enough to fuel up her love meter so she can share that love with others.

You're Called to Write When...

Linda Jewell

You figure out God called you to write when:

Your bucket list translates into writing projects.

You reread a draft of a story you wrote years ago, fall on your face, and whisper, "Thank You, Lord, for not allowing this to be published." However, you've learned a lot since your last edit and think, *Hmm, if I cut the first ten pages of backstory, and* . . .

Your spouse is getting ready for bed and calls out, "Remember, you have an early morning meeting at work tomorrow," and you're in front of your computer and answer, "I'm editing a scene. I'll be just a minute." Sixty minutes later, your spouse is snoozing peacefully, and you have one less hour to sleep until the alarm clock rings.

You tote polished drafts to critique group with high hopes and return home with copies covered with red marks because your put-a-comma-where-you-take-a-breath rule isn't working well with this crowd. Because you regret daydreaming when middle-school English teachers were teaching what-wasn't-important-to-you-then-but-is-now, you attend a college grammar class. You study hard and ask God to teach you what He wants you to learn. Your grade is irrelevant but what's important are four rules that address 80 percent of comma-required situations and a newfound confidence using them. Then the red-ink-slingers riddle your drafts with "POV" for point-of-view errors and they tell (not show) you, "Show-don't-tell."

Your sense of style reflects the latest edition of Chicago Manual of Style or The Associated Press Stylebook.

You tell people you're a writer because you put your seat in a chair and write.

You read how-to-write books during waiting-room time and keep a journal at your bedside so you can capture great lines of dialogue or plot twists in the middle of the night.

You've written for years but still celebrate every small success. Even if the odds are better you'll become an NFL player than a best-selling author, you keep writing.

You don't quit your day job.

Your head says it's not about fame or fortune yet your heart says it is. You eventually ask God to change your heart even if it means you earn less than minimum wage and your book is published after you die. You're no Olympic runner, but when you write you feel God's pleasure and you stay in the race, even if it's longer than 26.2 years. You're on your

70

face praying, "Not my will, but Yours, be done" because you're learning to trust God and His timing.

You send your babies-also-known-as-stories, out into the world with only a cover letter, and pray your words bring hope or help to readers you'll never meet face-to-face.

You give your friends a standing request for techno prayers. You have ongoing dialogue with God about open and shut doors. You see both as His loving kindness.

Your writing finally reflects the freedom of no longer pretending to be the kind of writer you're not.

You self-edit with the stout heart needed to chisel off words, chapters, chunks of purple prose, and mixed metaphors and you let them lay—no—lie on the cutting-room floor.

You beg God to open your eyes and ears and help you write all but only what He calls you to write and you submit to God by submitting your writing to editors for their consideration.

You write what you never thought possible, and experience God doing more than you can think or imagine, like when you receive a note from a stranger who doesn't know how to articulate her feeling to her family without the help of the words that flowed out of your heart, down your arms, and through your fingers to the keyboard.

You persist despite rejection letters or no response from editors while you're earning a doctorate in writing from the University of Hard Knocks.

You step out in faith, read guidelines, write a 750-word devotional about how to recognize God's call on your life, edit it, take it to critique group, edit, and submit it.

You remember the fires and rivers God has brought you through when you wavered and questioned, "God, did You really call me to write?" Then you'll write because, well, He called you to write.

If God called you to do something else besides write, you list all the ways His call has made a difference. And you'll answer His call with obedience and persistence, because, well, He called you.

Author and Perfecter of our faith, we ask You to pray for us and give us eyes to see, ears to hear, and a heart to obey Your call. We humbly ask for patience with Your perfect timing. Amen.

Linda Jewell writes and speaks about patriotism, parenting, and prayer. She supports troops and their families by encouraging home-front moms to develop brave hearts. She also volunteers with her church's Cookie Deployment.

Peace at Last

Carole Klock

When God first spoke to me about writing I protested, "Me?" I don't know anything about writing a book. Fifteen years in foster care is something I would rather erase from my memory. Writing about those experiences was never my desire. If I ever write my life story it will have to be a work of fiction, because no one will believe it. Besides, I didn't have the ability or talent.

For a time, I was a speaker for Stonecroft Ministries' Christian Women's clubs. My experiences as a foster child were the basis for my talk, but the message was how God had His hand on my life from the very beginning. Even when I thought I was abandoned, He was always there. I didn't understand that until I was older. I began to look back over the path I'd taken and as I shared my journey through those early years, I was surprised and humbled when I noticed women in the audience actually weeping.

My husband and I took a job managing a new self-storage site in San Diego in the year 2000. We split a twelve-hour work day. We had not been working the job long when the Lord spoke to my heart about writing my story. At first, I didn't believe it was Him speaking. But He would not leave me alone. Finally, I understood He wanted me to write my story. The very idea frightened me, and I pulled what I call a "Scarlett O'Hara." In the movie, *Gone with the Wind,* Scarlet dealt with things she couldn't handle by simply saying, "I'll think about that tomorrow." That's what I did.

Seven years flew by. My husband and I moved to Colorado Springs to manage another self-storage. Compared to the San Diego job, we were working bankers' hours.

Again, I felt that familiar tug on my heart. I imagined my Father standing with His arms crossed, tapping His toe. "I'm still waiting." I tried to argue and make excuses, but He said, "Do you realize you have disobeyed me for seven years?" I went into my bedroom one Sunday after church and got down on my knees. I told my Father I would try, but He would have to help me. Much of my story is traumatic and I did not want to remember. He gave me peace and let me know that I had a testimony and He wanted me to write it.

Writing the story was difficult. I found myself alternating between procrastinating and writing as if I could not get the words on the page fast enough. I put the writing away for months at a time. It took me ten years to write it. I never visualized actually finishing the story. But, one day, I did. It was 3:30 p.m. on a Thursday afternoon when I put the last period on the last sentence. I sat back in my chair and wept. I prayed and said, "Lord, I did it. I did what you asked." I was exhausted.

I attended a Bible study during that time. In the last lesson, the teacher shared that blessings to be received as a result of obedience to the Lord. She said, "Some of those blessings we anticipate, but He also has special gifts that we do not expect." I reflected on all of this and realized the teacher was correct. I noticed some changes in myself. God had worked a miracle, actually three miracles in me.

The baggage I had carried all those years was gone. For the first time in my life, I had complete peace. There was no guilt and no fear. The scars on my heart were not just healed over, they were gone. For years I had prayed, "Lord, you will have to forgive my foster mother and the man who sexually abused me, because I can't do it." The greatest of the three miracles that my Lord gave me was forgiveness. I just knew if those two people walked into the room, I would be able to say, "I forgive you," and mean it. I don't' have that opportunity because they are both deceased. But the fact is, I was the one most blessed because, I was free. I was a different person.

"For if you forgive men their trespasses, your
heavenly Father will also forgive you"
(Matthew 6:14 NKJV).

Carole Klock lives in Colorado with her husband, Harry. They recently celebrated sixty years of marriage. They have two sons and a daughter, seven grandchildren, and six great grandchildren. Carole is a quilter and very active in their church.

God's Miracle Plan

Marilyn Neuber Larson

When the phone rang my former sister-in-law said, "Mike had a catastrophic stroke. He's in the hospital and isn't expected to survive. I didn't want you to find out when you read his obituary in the newspaper."

What a shock.

My thoughts drifted back to our final troubled year when I prayed, "Dear Jesus, I'm terrified, is our marriage over? How can I survive? Lord, forgive me for my part in our relationship breakdown. Tell me what to do." That day I opened my Bible. "Trust in the Lord with all your heart, and lean not on your own understanding; in all your ways acknowledge Him and He shall direct your paths" (Proverbs 3:5-6 KJV).

Jesus seemed to whisper, "Trust me, Marilyn, I want you to trust me." I fell on my knees, confessed my sins, and gave my problems to him in prayer. Time went by and we worked on our problems and tried to restore our relationship—but it was not to be. On divorce day, I parked in a dark underground garage, climbed stairs to the street, and prayed. "Jesus, I'm not sure about this divorce." In brilliant sunshine a yellow-and-black Swallow-tail butterfly circled my head, as if to say, "Now watch me, Marilyn." It flew parallel to the courthouse, as if it followed a distinct path, then turned the corner and disappeared.

Trust me, Marilyn. In minutes, your life will turn the corner, but I will be with you. Jesus seemed to whisper, "I will never leave you or forsake you" (Hebrews 13:5 NKJV). My heart pounded and my knees trembled, but Jesus walked with me to my new life.

Now, as I sat in a stunned stupor, and my former husband faced death, a grateful memory came to mind.

Early in our marriage we had moved to Farmington for Mike's job, and while I worked in an insurance office, I met a new friend who was a secretary in the public schools. One day I said, "My degree is in elementary music, but Albuquerque does not employ music teachers in elementary schools."

Pauline interrupted, "But Farmington does—and we have an opening."

I landed that great job and taught music in two elementary schools. When the school year ended in May, Mike's company transferred us back to Albuquerque.

My principal said, "Marilyn, as soon as you get home, go to Albuquerque Public Schools and apply to teach an elementary class." "But I'm only qualified to each music," I said. He smiled. "Promise me, you will fill out an application. Just trust me and go."

On shaky legs, I obeyed.

Due to a teacher shortage, I was hired on the spot, on a conditional certificate. The condition: I must attend methods classes in summer school for two years. If I completed three classes: how to teach reading, math, and science, I would be qualified to teach a fourth-grade class in August. Next summer I'd take two classes to be fully qualified.

God called me to his miracle-plan for my life. Due to Mike's transfer to Farmington, I taught in elementary school, but if we had we refused to move, I doubt that I would ever have become a teacher.

So, as I thanked God and Mike for my thirty-two years in the classroom, I slept well.

The next day when the phone rang, Marcia said, "Mike died at 9:30 this morning." In shock, as I gazed through the window, a tiny white Cabbage Butterfly fluttered in the sunshine, and thoughts echoed from my life verse. "Trust in the Lord . . . and He shall direct your paths" (Proverbs 3:5-6 KJV).

Gratitude swept through me with an urgent need to thank God for every great, fun-loving year Mike and I shared before our path turned rocky.

"For I know the plans I have for you," declares
the Lord, "plans to prosper you and not to
harm you, plans to give you hope and a future"
(Jeremiah 29:11 NIV).

Dear Father, teach us how to totally trust you, no matter what, and thanks for your wonderful plan and call for our lives. Amen.

Marilyn Neuber Larson is a writer and speaker in Albuquerque, New Mexico. After her single years, she retired as an elementary teacher, married Bill, her pumpkin-farmer hero, and became the Pumpkin Queen.

Change of Plans – Funeral Canceled

Sharon Kern McCall

"Now it happened, the day after, that He went into a city called Nain; and many of His disciples went with Him, and a large crowd. And when He came near the gate of the city, behold, a dead man was being carried out, the only son of his mother; and she was a widow. And a large crowd from the city was with her. When the Lord saw her, He had compassion on her and said to her, 'Do not weep.' Then He came and touched the open coffin, and those who carried him stood still. And He said, 'Young man, I say to you, arise.' So he who was dead sat up and began to speak. And He presented him to his mother" (Luke 7:11-15 NKJV).

I am a planner who has been married for decades to my fabulous husband, Eddie, who is spontaneous and adventurous. These characteristics are wonderful; however, as an organizer, I find his traits challenging. It is not unusual for a family to arrive on our doorstep for dinner when I am completely unaware of Eddie's invitation to them. It is also common for him to decide on various exciting changes for our lives – exciting for him but interruptions for me.

We planners take great care to plan our days, careers, and lives. Many of us want a level of control, and we detest interruptions. It can be frustrating when life happens and our best laid plans are altered. However, when Christ interrupts our plans, we can be assured a blessing is ahead.

Let's embark on a journey with a woman from thousands of years ago who continues to teach us lessons today. Her name isn't revealed. She is only identified by the circumstances of her life and where she resides. We know she is a widow who lives in Nain.

This story begins at the gate of the city with two crowds of people whose lives intersected. Jesus was entering the city with a group of followers while a mourning funeral procession was leaving the city. These two groups met at the gate of the city of Nain. A young boy was being carried outside the city for burial. Jesus arrived at the gate of the city at an appointed time for His divine purpose on that designated day.

It is extremely painful for a mother to lose a child. As a widow, this mother was also depending upon her son to eventually provide for her during her aging years of life. She had already experienced the devastating loss of her husband and now she lost her only child. This mother was heartbroken and it was a time of immense sorrow. Although this grieving mother didn't ask Jesus to intervene, He demonstrated compassion for her and her situation. He responded to her weeping and her desperate condition. The Greek word for compassion that is translated in this passage refers to deep and inward emotions of pity and love. Jesus' response to this grieving mother was based on deep feelings He had for her and her plight in life. He called out to her and said, "Weep not" or "Don't cry." That would generally be impossible for a mother who was participating in her son's funeral procession and on her way to the cemetery. It was a time of extreme emotional pain and sorrow for this widow who was about to bury her only child. However, she had no idea what Jesus planned to do.

Jesus didn't always prevent the death of children nor did He respond to every grieving mother by raising her child from the dead. He chose this widow on this day for a specific purpose. He called her child from death to life. Her plan was to bury her only child. Jesus interrupted her plan and called her son to new life. Rather than grief and uncertainty about her future, she now had hope. Her son was alive. The final aspect of the funeral had been canceled. When Jesus calls and steps in, life as we have planned it, can be interrupted and altered to become totally renewed.

Heavenly Father, thank You for demonstrating your love and compassion for me. Thank You for caring enough about me to change my plans and replace them with Yours. Please help me to trust Your call on my life. In Jesus' name, Amen.

Sharon Kern McCall is a pastor's wife, mother, and grandmother with a passion for ministry to women. She has devoted her professional career of over 40 years to the Albuquerque Public Schools, University of New Mexico, University of New Mexico Hospital, and Wayland Baptist University. She has a PhD from the University of New Mexico and continues to prepare the next generation of educators.

GIVE ME A SIGN

SUSAN PARLATO REVELS

"Jessica was making funny faces at me so I was laughing. Teacher said to work but Jessica was making funny faces and I couldn't stop laughing." Andrew told me this in all his big-eyed seriousness from the chair in my office, the principal's office. He was supposed to be in trouble.

I had to do my best to not burst out laughing with pure pleasure. I couldn't do that. I was the principal after all. Would breaking into tears of joy be better?

This was the same little boy who at three years old, had finally heard for the first time with his new cochlear implants. The same boy who we wrung our hands over. The same boy whose parents met and planned and collaborated with us, with faces full of worry and hope. Could he learn to speak? Could he catch up with such a late start? Would he be able to read? In three years, he had gone from just able to imitate a vowel, to spilling out a 26-word sentence explaining his mischief. I just wanted to dance a jig!

Words, how we take them for granted. The rule system of sounds that gives way to connection with our fellow humans is dearly fought for everyday in my school, with the smallest of children. For each one it is a neurological emergency and the foundation for all relationships. If you cannot hear sound, the brain can never develop the auditory pathways for language, and you live with images and emotions and no way to intimately communicate them to another human. If language doesn't happen by seven years old, it may never happen.

"What really lights your fire?" my friend asked. "What is your calling?"

Hearing deaf children talk is my calling.

The journey started in tenth grade as I questioned my mother, "How did the deaf woman on Sesame Street learn to sign to those puppets?"

"I don't know," said Mom, and she booked an observation for me at a school for the deaf nearby.

That led me to decide, "I think I can do this the rest of my life."

College, graduate school, learning sign language, my first job in New York City, living in a deaf dorm were all milestones on the journey. A chance visit to Las Vegas kindled a love for the desert. Could God recreate that desert tranquility inside me, even though I lived in rainy, cold New York? "Bring me to a desert place, Lord." I meant could He do it in my heart. He did it in reality. A job in New Mexico got me packing my Cutlass Ciera and driving across country, alone, to a city sight unseen. Church introduced me to my future husband, a fellow interpreter in the deaf ministry. Time brought invention of mechanisms that initiated sound in the human brain. Providence brought me to a school that knew how to use those inventions. Work taught me how to interface that technology with the inner ear of a child. The silence of the mind is shattered with the first three small beeps, the child's response of surprise and wonder, and eventually vocalizations, words, and sentences. Language born, again, with each small child.

A pastor once said, "God wants us to bloom where we are planted. Our job becomes our harvest field. So it is for me. My journey has given me training in both the signing and spoken language arms of deaf education, a rare combination in the field. I have become a principal, a job I never dreamed of or expected, poised on the brink of change in the history of deafness and the ability to bridge two factions in the deaf world. Children's lives hang in the balance and I am consumed, "for such a time as this."

"How old are you Ms. Ann?"

"Well Andrew, I am 59 years old."

"Oh, you are old. You die soon."

"Well Andrew, I hope not too soon!"

"But that okay Ms. Ann. Because you die, then you see Jesus!"

A child, who first heard just three years ago, speaks The Word, to a captive world, and his voice echoes into eternity.

First Corinthians 2:9 says, "...Eye has not seen, nor ear heard, nor have entered into the heart of man the things which God has prepared for those who love Him."

Who would have imagined at 16 years old, passing by as my siblings watched Sesame Street, how that glimpse of an episode would impact my future? Who would have imagined what Andrew was capable of with that initial stimulation of sound to the auditory nerve? I am thankful for God's love and divine patience as each day unfolds the next part of his plan for me. If we can just trust Him with our lives and our futures, He will reveal the unimaginable in what He has prepared for each of us who love Him.

Susan Parlato Revels has a passion for teaching deaf children and fostering dialog about racial issues. Her interracial family lives in Albuquerque, New Mexico, and includes husband Scott, and children Cole and Gianina. www.bcausewecan.com; Facebook—BeCauseWeCan @ SusanParlatoRevels; email—bcausewecan2@gmail.com

Sock Monkey Christmas

Dan Rosecrans

Christmas, when I was a child, was delightful and simple. Oh, there were the trappings and trimmings, but it wasn't near as expansive as we see today. If you had asked me about "Black Friday" when I was young, my response would have linked America's great shopping day with the bubonic plague in England.

One of my fondest memories each year was when both sides of my family gathered for Christmas celebrations. My father's family came together on Christmas Eve. My mother's clan met on Christmas Day.

My father was the second oldest of six. Thus my siblings and I were blessed with a dozen cousins. The noise level at these Christmas Eve gatherings would have certainly rivaled a raucous sporting event in any arena. The adults tried to quiet the kids, all the while talking louder, which forced us to become even more boisterous. It was a delightful cycle resulting in an audacious cacophony of noise.

The shrill whistle of my Dad signaled it was time to eat. The bounty was modest, but wonderful. Each year the main dish was soup. There was chili, the Midwest kind with meat and beans, clam chowder and oyster stew. My Father, ever the sailor, loved the clams and oysters. Of course, every imaginable side dish and dessert found its way to the serving table. There was no worry about being last in line… my family brought plenty.

As the marvelous food settled in our stuffed bellies the noise level dropped a decibel or two. We kids were quieter as we knew the Christmas gifts would soon appear. Our tribe was so large that somewhere along the line the adults drew names. I never knew who I had or what I got anyone. Ah, the joy of being a child.

There was, however, one person we knew would always have something for each of her 15 grandchildren. Grandma Rosecrans lived on an extremely modest, fixed income. She was harshly stricken with arthritis in what seemed all her joints. But none were so obviously affected as the joints in her hands. Twisted and bent in unnatural ways she lived her days in extreme pain. Just doing the mundane daily tasks was, for her, excruciating.

Each year we all knew what we would receive from Grandma Rosecrans—sock monkeys. You may be familiar with them. Little labors of love which require time and dexterity even without arthritis. For my grandmother this must have been an unbelievably difficult and pain-filled task. While

I am certain some of my cousins appreciated the painstaking labor our grandmother put into these monkeys, I am ashamed to admit that the love she poured into each effort was lost on this young grandson. I remember quickly diverting my attention to another flashier toy to unwrap.

I was oblivious to the effort. I was oblivious to the disrespect and possible pain I caused the very woman who, with meager means and extreme pain, labored to make a memorable gift.

Life moved on at a frantic pace. My grandmother died. Only the youngest of my father's siblings survived. But the memory of the sights, sounds, and joy of those family gatherings have never been lost on me.

A few years ago, while experiencing some of the darkest days of my life, my older sister, Nancy, and I began talking about the long forgotten sock monkeys. I admitted my shame for being so thoughtless and ungrateful. A few days after our conversation, and my confession, I received a surprise package from my sister. It was, indeed, a sock monkey, one my sister had received from Grandma Rosecrans and kept for years. This priceless treasure - with a torn arm - reminded me of a woman who loved me and gave, though it, quite literally, hurt.

Simpler time, yes. Simple gifts, certainly. But gifts given with a heart and hand of love.

Perhaps every Christmas should once again be a thankful time for even the smallest gesture of love. Maybe these small gestures are actually the true and largest gifts we will receive. I have a sock monkey who taught me that lesson from long ago.

Thank you Father for even the smallest gifts of love.
Help us to receive them as from your very hand. Amen.

Dan Rosecrans lives in New Mexico where he and his wife, Laura, operate The HUB of New Mexico Christian Internet Station. Dan has been a communicator for 40 years serving and encouraging others with the hope of Christ. You can reach Dan at dan@thehubnm.com.

Are You That Person?

Laura Rosencrans

Sexual abuse, abortion, domestic violence—followed by rage, alcohol addiction, promiscuity, and divorce. These are the things that a good soap opera is made of; these are the things my own personal life involved. Growing up without my father who died when I was two, led me into a tailspin of searching for the love of a daddy who would protect me. Instead I found the abuse of a man who would shake my world and leave me a damaged 16-year-old.

Going into the Air Force to escape my past only got me more trouble. I became involved with the man who later became my first husband, another abusive relationship. My life continued on a downward spiral.

The good news is I accepted Jesus as my personal Savior in the midst of everything and I was able to receive His grace for all my sins—that is except one. I knew God could never forgive my abortion and I placed my baby above the Cross. Thirty-three years of pain torment and shame. Thirty-three years of being a believer who thought she could not be forgiven.

After 20 years of mental and emotional abuse, which I felt I deserved, the abuse turned toward one of our precious children, there are five; I knew it was time to go.

Then I married a man who was brought to me by God Himself. A man that made it his personal mission to help me find healing from my abortion and offered me the protection and love I had always desired. The same year we married, I went through an abortion healing class and I was set free. I finally accepted the forgiveness my Savior had given to me so many years ago.

And then it happened—God was able to use me to move into a ministry of helping other women find their forgiveness in Him. The funny thing is I had always told God I would never do ministry for women. I didn't like women. They were not safe to me. To be a friend you have to share life details and I knew I would be rejected. But I found out that was a lie of the enemy. Since I have come "out of the closet," so to speak, I have received nothing but love, grace, and encouragement to share my story so that I can be that safe person to others in pain.

Through the last few years of discovering my true identity in my Savior and my relationship with The Father I never had, I have studied much and one of my favorite books of the Bible is Job. I have to admit when I first read Job 1:8," Have you considered my servant Job?" spoken by God to Satan, I thought it was pretty lousy that here is a man who faithfully served God and was righteous and yet God pointed him out to Satan.

But God has given me the understanding of why He did so. Job's faithfulness, gave God faith in him. So much so that He knew Job would never fail. He questioned and faltered at times but He never ever gave up on God. God even wrote an entire book on Job in His Word as a shining example to us all about what it means to have that kind of faith in our Father.

So now instead of asking "Why God?" I ask myself— Am I that person that God will say to Satan "Have you considered my daughter Laura?" Am I that person God will have faith in knowing that I will stand faithful and true to Him? Am I that person that God will proudly acknowledge that He knows that no matter what has happened in my life with all its trials and muck, I will not fail because I serve a God who will never fail me?

What about you, my friend, "Are you that person?"

Father God, I pray for my brother or sister reading this that they will be that person that God is able to say, "Have you considered my servant _____". Give them the strength and endurance to accept the challenge no matter the circumstance they are facing. Amen.

Laura Garcia-Rosecrans is a writer and speaker. An advocate/coach to women who have experienced traumas in life - she journeys with them to discover their true identity in Christ. Alongside her husband Dan, they own The HUB of New Mexico Christian Internet Radio

Station speaking life into a dark world. She can be reached at laura@thehubnm.com.

CALLED TO TRUST GOD

MYKAELA SAVAGE

Let's be honest. We all have issues. Mine is trusting God. I don't trust Him when He says I'm saved and secure in His hand. It's a constant battle for me. I know what He says in the Bible about my salvation, but still, I doubt. And it took a kick in the pants for me to finally understand what God is calling me to do during my trial. He is calling me to trust Him.

I hear God call as He places certain verses and sermons in my path that speak to my specific struggle. He gives those I love the right words to say at the right moment. He takes away my tendency to control the situation and helps me to trust in His power so that through Him, I can be healed.

I think trust is something we all struggle with at some point or another. When it seems impossible to overcome struggles and nothing good can ever come of it, God still calls us to trust in His plan. Jeremiah 29:11 says, "'For I know the plans that I have for you,' declares the Lord.

'Plans for peace and not for evil, plans to give you a future and a hope.'" (ESV) This is the promise God gives to us all, and all we have to do is trust Him. But how do we have faith in Him during a storm?

A great place to look would be the Bible. Go ahead, roll your eyes and say, "That's the most cliché thing I've ever heard, and I hear stuff like that all the time." But think about it for a moment. How many people do we see in the Bible who have been through the fire?

Esther is a great example of trust in God. I love Esther because, being a young girl myself, I can relate to her struggle of understanding God's plan when her life was at stake. While my life has never been on the line, I have failed in my calling to hope in the Lord. Esther is a great role model for me. She's a young, pretty, teenager forced to compete in a beauty contest, in a land where her people are captives, and made a queen.

Not long after, her uncle Mordecai uncovers a plot to kill the Jews, Esther's people. Mordecai pleads with Esther to go and expose the plot to the king. As Esther walks into the king's presence uncalled for, she knew it could cost her her life.

You think Esther was enthralled or excited with this idea? No. I bet she was fearful, confused. I bet she looked up at the sky and said, "God, I don't understand. Why me?" She had no clue what was going on, but trusted God anyway. She fasted. She prayed. And she went.

Esther understood that God must have some plan, or He wouldn't call her to do this. Her faith in was God strong enough that she could say, head held high, "If I perish, I perish." (ESV)

The Bible is full of stories like Esther's. But what do all those people have in common? Their call to trust God, sometimes with their lives. Did they understand? Nope. Were they always happy? I'd be concerned for their sanity if they were. Yet, they knew that God was good and hoped in His Word.

This life is full of challenges, and it can be hard to trust God when we're standing in the fire. Whatever our struggle or doubt, we find ourselves shaking our fist at the sky screaming, "Why, God?" because we don't understand. We want Him to take away our struggle, and sometimes miss what God calls us to during those trials. He calls us to trust Him.

So, when you're standing in the fire, remember those from the Bible who trusted God in the trials. Remember those who are standing beside you. Know that God is bigger than you, and His plan is for your good. God promises that in the Bible, and He never lies. Ever. Go back to Jeremiah 29:11 as many times as it takes, and answer God's call when He asks you to trust Him.

Dear Lord, I pray for strength to answer the call to trust You. I ask for forgiveness where I have doubted and tried to take control. Please give me faith. Amen.

Mykaela Savage lives with her family in Brownsboro, Texas, where she pursues her passion for writing.

Called to a Journey

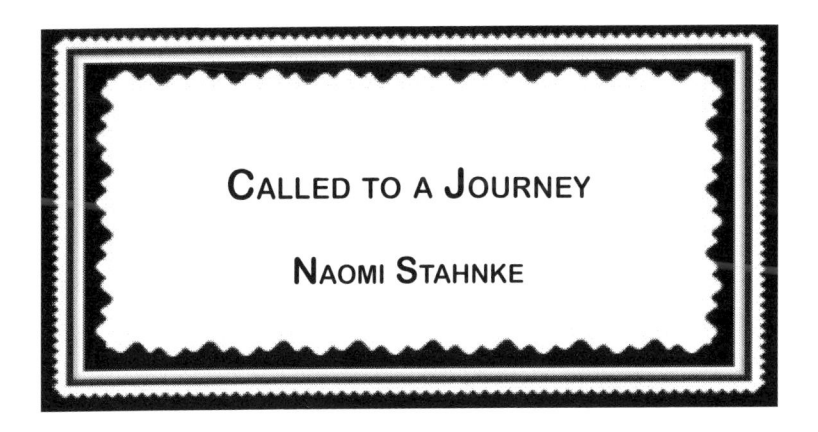

Naomi Stahnke

"I am sure of this, that He who started a good work in you will bring it to completion at the day of Christ Jesus" (Philippians 1:6 ESV).

My calling from God was never a distinct, "Naomi! I have called you and made you to be a writer! Go forth and write great stories that share my love!" Although that might have been nice, especially since I have a personality that likes to be prepared and know everything that is going to happen as far ahead as possible. But God didn't do it that way.

Neither did He make it obvious from the beginning, creating a desire to write from an early age. I was fourteen before I decided that writing was not a torture device introduced to the school system sometime during World War II.

But I love to look back and see how, little by little as I have grown up, God has revealed who He has made me to be. It started when I was just a little girl, reading entire novels in a day and playing with my imaginary friends for hours on end. Little did I know those novels were laying the groundwork for my talent with words, and those imaginary friends would grow up to take a special place in my heart and the hearts of my readers.

Then came the thunderous first year and a half between my acknowledgment that I loved to write and my first published novel. As always, it was my mom who really pushed me to explore my gifts and actually finish a project. Throughout the writing process of that first book, God really established what I was to do with my life; where my talents and gifts were to be found.

Two novels and a couple devotionals later, I'm still battling self-doubt and fear. Yet God never fails to gently correct me, reaffirming His call each and every day. Best of all, I can't even begin to guess at the amazing things He is preparing me to do!

God's calling for me has been more of a step-by-step, one-exciting-discovery-at-a-time sort of relationship. I think He's done it this way because a calling is more than just a job description given by a distant Deity. A calling is the real you, the beautiful, unique person He envisioned at creation. Finding your calling is not so much a one-time download from God, but an intimate, lifelong journey with Him. A lifelong journey that I'm still just at the beginning of, but so excited to continue!

Dear Father, Thank you for the calling you have placed on my life! I pray that you will continue to reveal your plans to me, helping me to be patient and wait for your timing. I am so honored and excited to walk this journey with you. Have Your way in my life! Amen.

Naomi Stahnke is eighteen years old and lives with her parents and three adopted siblings in Northern Colorado. She is the author of two novels, *The Blue Feather Escape* and *To Be Free*. In addition to fiction writing, she enjoys writing devotionals, worship dance, and adapting and directing church plays.

FLY LIKE AN EAGLE

DIANE STELTER

A few years ago, I visited my daughter and her family while they were stationed in Alaska. What beautiful country! I was impressed by the snowcapped mountains, the water, the wildlife. Crazy looking birds, moose roaming the streets, fish jumping high out of the water, it was like a zoo with no fences. Everywhere I looked, another wildlife surprise amazed me.

While on our way to the local Safeway grocery, on the corner of a busy intersection, there in a barren field was a dead tree with an eagle's nest on top of it.

No covering at all, it was subject to all of the elements. The eagle perched, looking majestic hovering over the nest, protecting it's young.

It's been almost three years since that visit and I don't think of it often. But recently, as I was praying, God brought it back as a reminder of how He cares for me.

It's my prayer that God will show me clearly His will for my life. I don't care what it is, I just want to see it, know it, and do it. As I was pleading once again for Him to guide me and give me the ability to clearly see His call, He opened my eyes to something I had never thought about.

Instantly, I saw a nest and baby bird. Somehow, I knew the baby bird was an eagle and I knew it was me. I watched as two HUGE hands placed this baby right in the center of the giant nest, just like the one I saw in Alaska. All sticks and leaves, no covering, exposed to the elements. This bird was a homely little thing, mouth wide open, pleading for food. He was not ready to fly and even if he wanted to, the nest was so big and protective, he most likely couldn't get the edge.

This is when God seemed to say…'You're not ready to fly into my plans for you. This is a safe place to grow, learn and experience care *exclusively* from me, just like the baby eagle only knows the care of it's parents. This nest is very high above the ground and if you try to leave too soon, you will crash. Although it feels like you are in a barren place, exposed to the elements, you must trust me to be your protection. One day you will soar, but for now you are growing strong wings to hold you up during the trials of life."

Just as young eaglets learn by imitating their parent, we learn by imitating our Father. Ephesians 5:1 MSG says, "Watch what God does, and then you do it, like children who learn proper behavior from their parents." As a mother eagle knows its time for her eaglet to fly, she makes the nest uncomfortable so they want and need to leave. Do you think God also creates discomfort in our lives to help us grow and mature?

The truly beautiful thing is that even when it's time to leave the nest, the mother never loses sight of her child. As the baby eagle topples over the side and begins descending downward, Mama swoops in and lifts the bird, carrying it on her wings. She will do this over and over until the eaglet gains confidence and has strong enough wings to soar above the clouds.

I know the feeling of being stuck in that great big nest, with no ability to see over the edge. It's prickly and stinky and at times, suffocating. But I have come to realize that my time in the nest is not wasted and neither is yours. We are building our muscles, we're gaining strength and learning to trust our Father God for everything.

Do you want to soar above your circumstances? Are you ready to launch out and fly into all that God has for you? I know that I do, so I'm going to stay here in my nest,

the one prepared just for me and learn all that I can so when it's my turn to take flight,

I'm ready.

> "Those who hope in the Lord will renew their strength. they will soar on wings like eagles. They will run and not grow weary, they will walk and not faint" (Isaiah 40:31)

Diane Stelter resides in Holland, Michigan, with her husband Jim and precious pooch, Brody. Mother of 4 and grandmother of 10, she is also a salon owner, stylist, and

Certified Personality Trainer and speaker. Her silver hair and pink roots are her trademark identifying mark.

DREAD BECOMES JOY

CHARLOTTE WHEAT

Fire and brimstone preaching swirled around my young head every time I went to church. The preachers pounded the pulpit, grew red in the face, sweated, shouted, cried, begged people to "come to Jesus before it is too late." At home, we had a set of Old Testament Bible Stories, not especially written for children. But I read them over and over. Like Job I heard of God but I did not know Him.

At the age of nine I craved peace of mind. Shame and guilt haunted me. I remember one Sunday morning I stepped forward with shaky knees, confessed Jesus' name before others and repented of the lies and other things Mother reminded me of. I chose Jesus as my Savior and Lord, goaded by the fear of God and the dread of hell. I came up out of that baptistry with such relief it made me giddy. I was safe! But I knew from past teaching that I had to stay in the straight and narrow to remain that way.

I did not feel the love of God, did not understand grace, knew nothing about the comforter, the Holy Spirit.

This brought me to ought-to works done by my will and strength rather than want-to service done with the Spirit's power and guidance. I set myself up to burn out or fall away.

While in the fifth grade, a wonderful Sunday School teacher taught us about the love of Jesus. Her gentleness with this rough-edged girl demonstrated such love. Ministers at church camp reinforced her teachings. They filled my ten-year-old heart with a better understanding of Jesus and I no longer feared God. Can't say I was filled with love, but maybe respect and an urge to serve Him in a special way. One Friday night, in an open-air chapel, with the cicadas buzzing and kids singing I walked forward and dedicated myself to full-time Christian service. From then on, I surrendered to God and Christ.

Later, Sunday School teachers asked me to play the piano for the children's department in the church's basement every Sunday until I was in the eighth grade. Then I started playing for the service upstairs. I sang in the youth choir and my twin brother and I sang duets for the church service occasionally. Now, I question if the joy I felt in this kind of service fed my pride or showed an inkling of growing love for God and His Son.

In high school, I prepared for my calling by enrolling in choir to train my voice, shorthand to take notes in class, Latin to help with Greek, and speech to make me a better teacher and speaker. I assumed leadership roles in our youth group and played the piano for everything at church. During my last year at church camp, I loved a class called, Directing Congregational Singing. A girlfriend and I entered a preaching contest held for the boys (shook the preachers up).

Always in touch with Christ and our Father yet not real close, I belonged to a Bible Club all through high school, went to youth rallies and taught a four- and five-year-old Sunday School class my senior year.

At Ozark Bible College in Joplin, Missouri, I met and married my husband, W. A., a senior preparing to be a minister. Later, I took some kids to junior church camp as a sponsor. I don't remember the sermon on a Wednesday night but it convicted my heart and soul. To keep the girls from hearing me cry, I cried into my pillow, with sorrow over my years of misunderstanding God. But the Holy Spirit moved me to cry with joy over my peace in Christ. Finally, my dread became joy because of His Spirit filling me.

Dear Father, lead us to understand your grace and mercy and find true peace and joy." I had heard of You[only] by the hearing of the ear; but now my [spiritual] eye sees You" (Job 42:5 AMP).

Charlotte Wheat, a retired teacher, lives in Lubbock, Texas, with her husband, W. A., a retired minister. Ask her about their three children and grandchildren. Called to write, teach, and encourage, Charlotte serves with want-to joy.

REVELATIONS ON A HIKING TRAIL

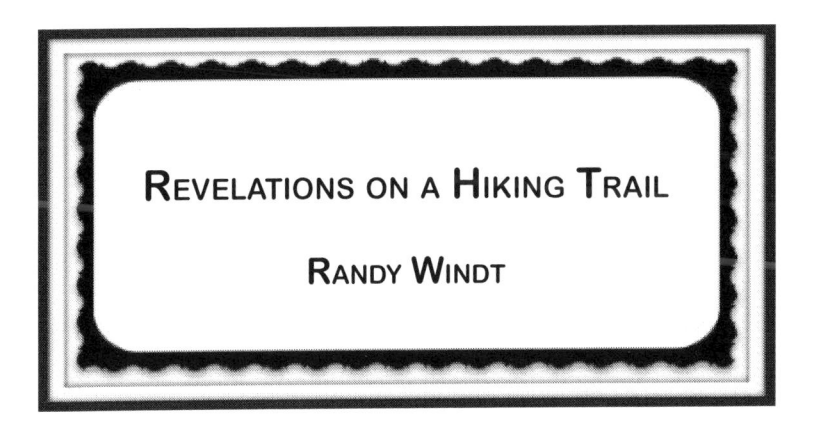

RANDY WINDT

I shall never forget it. Having recently been born again, I passionately devoured the Word of God, spending every possible spare moment in it as God increasingly opened my eyes to behold the beauties and wonders of His truths as revealed in the holy Scriptures.

One glorious afternoon in which the creation declared the glory of the Creator of heaven and earth, I walked along a hiking trail high up in the Catalina Mountains north of Tucson, Arizona, pondering the doctrine of double imputation. For as beautiful as nature was that day, with the endless views of pine trees, the beautiful overlooks of the desert below, the glistening sun, and the crisp air, it was not worthy to be compared to what occurred in my inward man. I could not get over my meditations on how all of my sins had been credited to Christ, and that He, as my perfect, spotless, sinless substitute, paid their full penalty at Calvary's Cross. As Horatio Spafford penned in his timeless hymn, "It is Well with My Soul," it was a blissful thought indeed to ponder that "my sin, not in part, but the whole, is nailed to the cross, and I bear it no more." I could see Christian, the main character in John Bunyan's classic book, The Pilgrim's Progress, making his way up the hill which led to the Cross with a heavy burden on his shoulders. When he reached the Cross, that burden fell off his shoulders, "and [he] saw it no more."

But my musings did not stop there. I had come to see that not only had my sins been imputed/counted/reckoned to Christ, but that God had credited His perfect righteousness to my account.

"How can this be?" I wondered. My righteousness is but filthy rags in the sight of a perfectly holy and righteous God, Who now, by grace through faith in Christ, removed and replaced those wretched, stained rags with a new, spotless robe of perfect righteousness. Consider the story of Joshua the high priest in Zechariah 3: "Joshua was standing before the angel, clothed with filthy garments. And the angel said to those who were standing before him, 'Remove the filthy garments from him.' And to him He said, 'Behold, I have taken your iniquity away from you, and I will clothe you with pure vestments.' And I said, 'Let them put a clean turban on his head.' So they put a clean turban on his head and clothed him with garments" (Zechariah 3:3-5). Just as He did for Christian in The *Pilgrim's Progress*, and for Joshua the high priest, God stripped me of my rags and gave me a change of raiment. My only possible response could be that of Isaiah: "I will greatly rejoice in the LORD; my soul shall exult in my God, for He has clothed me with the garments of salvation; He has covered me with the robe of righteousness, as a bridegroom decks himself like a priest with a beautiful headdress, and as a bride adorns herself with her jewels" (Isaiah 61:10).

Thoughts like these filled my heart and mind that incredible day on the hiking trail in the Catalina Mountains. I felt as if I would burst with excitement as the Lord filled my cup to overflowing with unspeakable joy. But then another thought intruded into my thinking; these glorious gospel truths are not meant only for me. I shouldn't hide them under a basket. Indeed, Jesus commanded His disciples to "go into all the world and proclaim the gospel to the whole creation" (Mark 16:15).

On that day, in the midst of a pine forest, I asked the Lord if He was calling me to a life of service for the advancement of His Kingdom in the role of a teacher of His Word. Since that day, it consumes me with passion. I have since experienced many ups and downs, many doubts, many fears, but God has sustained me through it all. May He continue to do so!

After that day on the hiking trail, I have learned that above all else, God must be our chief delight. When we come to the realization that nothing can separate us from His love, it is only then that we can be content in whatever circumstances His providential hand might place us.

O most precious, merciful, loving Lord, thank you for taking our sins upon Yourself and giving us Your perfect righteousness. In Jesus' Name. Amen.

Randy Windt is a Bible teacher. Soli Deo gloria!

CALLED TO SERVICE

JAMES WININGER

> "I thank Him who has given me strength,
> Christ Jesus our Lord, because He judged me
> faithful, appointing me to His service"
> (1 Timothy 1:12 ESV).

I've often wondered what prompted me to begin writing. I now know it was God's gift to a young man He created and had plans for. As a young boy, I made my way into the nearby woods with a pencil and a tablet of paper I saved up for by salvaging pop bottles along the roadside. I wrote myself into various stories based on books I had read or adventures I dreamed of having. For me, writing was an escape from a less than happy childhood.

As I grew, I wrote poetry to express my feelings of hopelessness, sadness, and discouragement. I sometimes wrote dark stories of abuse, deceit, and death. Most often, I wrote of happy adventures and dreamscapes that took me away from the realities of my early life. I squirreled away my writing by placing it into a hole in the wall of the house I lived in; and there between the wall studs I stored my private dreams of escape. I considered these wistful dreams my treasures and guarded them carefully.

Through the years, I continued writing as an outlet to express my innermost thoughts and feelings. I seldom ever shared any of them because the one time I did, with an older half-brother, I was ridiculed and again told how stupid and useless I was, and how I would never amount to anything. So I kept my writing to myself; it was safer that way. In my teens, I found my way to Christ through God's amazing grace on a fall evening in 1975.

Shortly after that wonderful, life-changing experience, I found my writing changed. I stopped writing about fanciful dreams and adventures and started writing about my life experiences as I matured. There were still times when I dwelt on my turbulent past and wrote about my negative feelings, but I soon realized that writing about God—and the wonderful new experiences He was bringing to my life—was much more my focus. I still kept much of my writing to myself as scars from my childhood were still very real. After my military service, college, and marriage, I continued writing, but the quantity had greatly decreased. I rediscovered my passion for writing as I felt more joy in developing the user manuals for the software I developed in my small business than I had in developing the software itself. In time, I turned my passion for writing into a career as a technical writer and later formed capture and proposal writing teams for various companies.

I came to understand that while my writing was personal, I was inspired to begin sharing the words I used to express my life with others. Sometimes I displayed something I wrote on the walls of my office or on my whiteboard. Other times, I created presentations, wrote articles, and submitted papers that helped to educate, encourage, and compel others to pursue their goals and dreams. Still, poetry, devotionals, and worship were the majority of my writing. I kept these private and only shared them sparingly until after I retired and resumed the rural lifestyle I had grown to miss so much.

During one of my morning prayers—while sitting atop a hill at the western edge of my ranch where I often devote my day to Christ as the sun rises—God called me to His service. On that morning, God reminded me of His words in Deuteronomy 6:9; "You shall write them on the doorposts of your house and on your gates" (NKJV), which led me to begin sharing my thoughts for His glory. I began writing devotionals to my Lord in earnest, and started teaching lessons during Sunday evening worship services at our little country church. Today, I prayerfully thank my Savior for His encouragement to use the gifts He gave me, in His service.

Until called home to glory, I will dedicate my writing to Abba, my friend, my all.

J. D. Wininger is an experienced, award-winning business writer and speaker. Semi-retired, when not tending his cattle with his sidekick Diogi (D-O-G) or doing chores, Jim spends time researching, discovering, and glorifying his Lord.

MORE THAN BIRDS

RICHELLE WRIGHT

My excitement was rising—today was more than special. I've been called by God to minister to women in jail and prison. I sat in my car waiting for the rest of my team to arrive before beginning our morning of ministry. I prayed as I waited. *Lord give us a special word for Your daughters who are on the inside. May our words be Yours and may we be proper examples of You as we minister.*

As I joined the other three ladies of my team, I noticed their exhilaration about several birds splashing in a puddle of water near the entrance of the corrections facility. The birds acknowledged us; how close we were, marveling at their enjoyment. They seemed not to care. While the ladies giggled with glee, I took a chance. I inched close enough to touch the birds and asked, "Good morning, friends. Would you please whistle a tune for us?" To our amazement, they obliged. I turned to my teammates, "See the happiness they have about how God provided a pool for them to bathe in? The Lord is faithful even to these birds by tending to their needs."

We made our way to the entrance, signed in, and processed through to our unit, and finally our assigned community pod. Giddy to see us, the ladies quickly helped arrange the room for our group discussion about worry. Once settled, we asked the ladies, "What do you worry about?"

We went around the room; the tension mounted. The first woman spoke. "I worry about what will happen during my court date."

The second said, "I worry that my kids are safe while I'm in here. I miss them with all my heart and want to be home."

Still a third stated, "I worry if I even have a place to call home when I get out of here." A low murmur of affirmation, followed by a heavy silence filled the room as if these inmates were longing to be anywhere, anywhere, but behind bars.

The Lord reminded me of the birds. My team shared with the ladies how God provided for the birds we saw at the entrance of the building. Each of us gave our own account about the bird bath serenade that took place prior to our jailhouse meeting.

I summarized, "God's Word tells us in Matthew 6:25-34 not to worry about what we eat, drink, or wear. God already knows what we need. He's already in the future working everything together for our good. What we should do instead of worry is what verse 33 instructs us, "Seek first the kingdom of God and His righteousness" and He will add everything we need.

Our birds' symphony showed they weren't worried about where the water came from or where the water would be in two hours; they enjoyed the bath in the moment. If the Lord provided water for the birds to bathe, how much more will He provide for you?" Within seconds, enthusiasm returned, chasing away tension and heaviness. Wow. In that instant, I realized today was special indeed.

Take a lesson from the birds. Have you ever seen a bird worry? Why should you? If God takes good care of the birds, He'll take even better care of you.

Loving Father, thank You for Your faithfulness to provide for even the birds who do not worry about their future. I won't worry either. Instead, help me to seek You in the moment so You can provide my needs. Amen.

Richelle Wright—a humble worshiper, intercessor, skilled teacher, lover of God. From her own traumatic experiences, her heart yearns to help hurting women heal and overcome that they may experience the fullness of God's blessings.

WHERE ARE THE REST

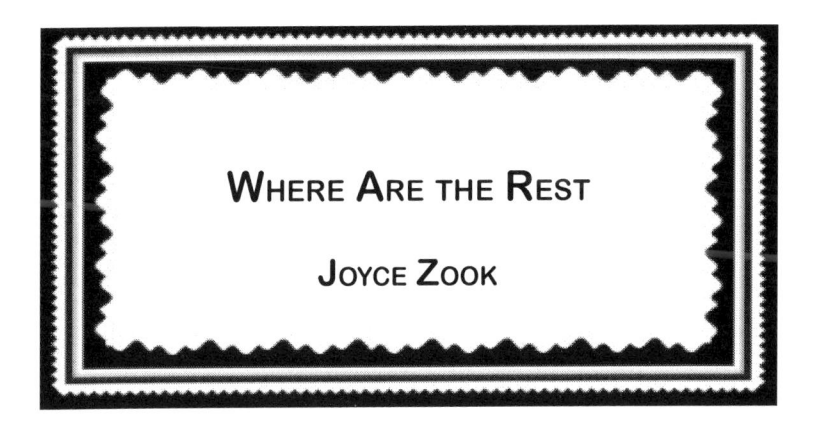

JOYCE ZOOK

"Bye, Mom," the boys yelled as they ran to catch the early morning bus for their hour-long ride on the autobahn. Ten years of homeschooling and now we sent them off to high school. What a shock not to have them around 24/7.

We lived on a British NATO base in Germany and our sons' school was in Schinnen, Netherlands. Teaching our sons had been wonderful for us as an Army family, but we couldn't pass up the opportunity for our teenagers to experience an International Department of Defense (DOD) school.

Classes with students from twenty-three different nations. Sporting events in England and Belgium. Swimming in the Olympic pool in Munich and a weeklong trip to study and see musicals in London. These would be experiences of a lifetime.

After the bus left, I stood alone in my dining room alone and stared at my British garden. I wondered, "No kids, no school. What do I do now?"

Suddenly, I was caught up into heaven. It felt surrealistic, like a vision. I stood in a short line, in the middle of a cloud. Everything around me glowed in the palest of grays. It wasn't quiet, yet I couldn't identify the sounds.

When I got to the front of the line, a man I didn't recognize sat at a white table with a large file box. He looked up and said, "Hi, Joyce."

"Now that's interesting, He knew my name. Was He the Lord?

He riffled through the cards until He found mine and tilted it forward to see what was behind it. He smiled and He looked at me. "I see you led your sons to Me. Well done. You are a good and faithful servant."

His brow wrinkled and He raised His eyebrows as He studied the cards behind mine. He looked up and said, "Where are the rest?"

"What do you mean?" I said.

"You are not done just because you led your sons to Me. Go. Spend the rest of your life telling these people about My love."

"Who are these people?"

"They are the women I planned for you to bring to Me."

Back in my dining room, I stood still, not wanting to lose the moment. "Was that real?" Tears came to my eyes. God called me to be a wife first, then a mom and a homeschooling mom. I thought my purpose ended when the boys went to high school, but God had a new mission for me.

Later, the Lord explained the vision He had given me. He whispered in my ear, "Love My sheep, teach My sheep, lead My sheep."

"What do You mean?" I said.

He said, "Love the women I put before you. Share my love. Pray for them. Care for them and let them know how much I love them.

"Teach these women, young and old, about Me. Teach them My truths and promises. Show them how to live by My principles in their everyday lives. Show them how to work together.

"Lead women wherever I put you, in groups and individually. Be their example. Show them how I heal and forgive through your own life. Mentor the younger wives. Help them find joy and peace in Me, as you have."

The Scriptures speak to older women saying, "Train the younger women to love their husbands and their children, to live wisely and be pure, to work in their homes, to do good, and to be submissive to their husbands." (Titus 2:4-5 NLT).

Who has God called you to love, teach, and lead; your kids, coworkers, those in a ministry where you serve, or in your community?

Lord, help me tell others about You, the One who always keeps His promises, always forgives us and never guides us in the wrong direction. Amen

Joyce Zook is the award-winning author of *12 Keys for Marriage Success*, *Priorities for Life,* and *God and Your Closet.* She is an International Speaker and Life and Marriage Coach. Find out more at JoyceZook.com.

Called to Encourage

Lessie Harvey

Preparation for knee replacement surgery was a breeze. Since I had already had one knee replacement surgery, I knew what to expect and was not afraid. The only thing I needed was prayer, lots and lots of prayer to cover me before, during, and after surgery. My family, friends, church, and everyone who knew me had prayed. I felt protected.

The knee replacement surgery went well. My first task was to sit in a chair for 45 minutes, which I did that for 40 minutes before I felt dizzy. I remember pushing the nurse call button and telling her how I felt. The next thing I remember is about 20 people running down the corridor pushing me in my bed.

"What's your name? Where are you?"

"Lessie. I'm in the hospital. Why?"

"Where were you?" asked a doctor I had never seen before.

"In my room until y'all came," I responded. What a stupid question I thought because I didn't understand why all these people were around me.

I learned I had coded. Even with that knowledge, I wasn't afraid because I genuinely believed God would take care of me because that's the prayer we had prayed.

"Have I not commanded you? Be strong and courageous. Do not be afraid; do not be discouraged, for the LORD your God will be with you wherever you go" (Joshua 1:9 NIV).

I love reading God's encouraging words. They strengthen and boost my confidence to move forward, despite my reservations. My circumstances or situations may not change, but my courage and commitment to continue moving forward, believing God is faithful to His Word, shows me He is the same yesterday, today, and tomorrow.

Trusting God to keep His Word and experiencing the fruit of trusting Him in my life uplifts me. As with all good things that happen to me, I want to share. Therefore, my desire is to encourage and strengthen others using God's Word. To walk beside them during difficult times, listen to their concerns, pray for them, and ask God to give me a word of encouragement for them. They may or may not immediately respond, but in God's timing, they accept and believe His Word. Together we rejoice in God's goodness.

Speaking a word of encouragement to those who are burdened is like resuscitating a person who has been overwhelmed by life's obstacles. Empowering words refresh the soul, strengthen the body, and uplift the spirit. To me, godly words of wisdom are like Jesus breathing His Holy Spirit into people, who are then equipped and enabled to overcome that which once bound them.

Is this your experience? Who has God used to inspire and strengthen you? Or who has God allowed you to build up through uplifting words? Have you witnessed the life-giving power of encouraging words, especially to those who are hopeless?

Isaiah 6:8 says, "Then I heard the voice of the Lord saying, 'Whom shall I send? And who will go for us?' And I said, 'Here am I. Send me!'"

When God answers my prayers and brings me through life's difficulties, I share what He has done for me. That's how I feel I am sent like Isaiah. Do you want to share what God does in your life? Someone needs to hear how He has answered your prayers, brought you through difficult circumstances, or boosted your confidence when you wanted to give up. Your words of encouragement are exactly what someone needs to hear to believe God can do the same for them.

Father, You know the heart and needs of Your people. Please use me to speak encouraging words to those who need to hear them. Amen.

Lessie Harvey lives in Maryland with her husband, Jesse. Her three adult children and grandchildren are near enough to fuel up her love meter so she can share that love with others.

Rough Wooden Boxes

Linda Jewell

I cried for months after our son, Ty, moved away and my husband, Jim, and I became empty nesters. One Saturday morning, I tackled the weekly house cleaning while Jim ran errands. I stepped out of Ty's former bedroom and heard a voice overhead say, "Write."

Startled, I looked up at the skylight directly above me. *Is Jim on the roof? Has he taken off the skylight to pull a prank on me?*

I shook my head. *What am I thinking? I'd never seen my serious-minded husband on the roof. I'm losing my mind. Missing Ty so much is getting to me.*

A few Saturdays later, after dusting our son's room, I stepped under the same skylight. I again heard a voice above me say, "Write."

My soul knew God was speaking to me.

In the following year, tears fell each time I told God I didn't feel worthy of His call. "What could I ever write that would be good enough for You?" I'd say. "You created the universe, the sun, the moon, and the stars. You own the cattle on a thousand hills. Besides, You wrote the bestseller of all times."

A month of Saturdays later, I wandered into Ty's deserted bedroom. In the bookcase the blue cover of Charles Tazewell's *The Littlest Angel* caught my eye. One of my favorite stories, I'd given a copy to our son the Christmas he was six.

Sunlight streamed though windows. I sat on the floor with knees pulled up, back against the bed, and read again the story about heaven's angels being in a dither about the arrival of the Christ Child. Amidst the splendid gifts to the Babe, the littlest angel humbly gave his most precious possessions in a rough wooden box. This gift God transformed into the Star of Bethlehem.

I closed the book, blotted tears with my sleeve, and surrendered. "Okay, God, if You want my rough wooden box, my writing, You can have it." I considered possibilities. "What do You want me to write?"

It didn't matter at that point. I took my best attempt at a magazine article, all twelve pages of a very rough draft, to a critique group. The first page was so bad one woman didn't know where to begin. "This doesn't have flow," she said. A young man explained that one idea should connect to the next, like a string of pearls. That day in critique group I also learned something about God's sense of humor. He didn't call me to write because I could, but because I couldn't. However, I had no doubts He had called me to write, so I persisted despite lack of talent or success. I also attended classes, conferences, seminars, webinars, and critique groups and read books about the craft of writing. God in His mercy gave me the ability to see my areas of ignorance as opportunities to learn more about writing and more about Him.

God also encouraged me with small successes. Just as a kind word holds the power to motivate us for years, I became encouraged whenever a publisher accepted one of my stories.

These days, knowing God has called me to write helps me work in His strength, not mine. I have limited control over whether or not a publisher chooses what I submit. Having learned more about the craft, I'm thankful some earlier pieces were not published. I do pray for God's favor with editors, but I no longer see rejection slips as indication of my worth. Rather, they motivate me to self-edit, protect writing time, learn to become more proficient, study markets, and submit projects to publishers for their consideration.

Writing filled my empty nest. It also helped me give my husband grace because I no longer resented the time he watched sports on TV. Instead I became grateful for opportunities to slip into my office, Ty's former bedroom, and write. And, in a way only God could arrange, twenty-five years after God called me to write, our now retired military son and I are talking about working together on a writing project.

Hopefully, each of God's people will heed His call. Even if our imperfect gifts are like the Littlest Angel's rough wooden box, God can transform them into lights that shine so brightly they will lead others to Christ.

Dear Jesus, thank You for the grace and gift of Your call. Amen.

Linda Jewell writes and speaks about patriotism, parenting and prayer. She supports troops and their families by encouraging home-front moms to develop brave hearts. She also volunteers with her church's Cookie Deployment.

HE HAS A PLAN

GERRY WAKELAND

It was a hot, humid June morning as we gathered in the church sanctuary for the closing ceremony of Vacation Bible School. The children sang, and the pastor gave a moving message. Then he asked, "Does anyone here want to give his or her heart to Jesus?" He stepped from the pulpit and waited for the someone to come forward.

I was twelve years old and had given my heart to Jesus when I was seven. But that morning I felt something strange happen inside of me. It's hard to describe, but somehow I knew that God was trying to tell me something.

All week we had heard stories about missionaries who had given their lives to share the Gospel around the world. We were inspired by tales of Lottie Moon in China and Jim Elliot who was killed by the Auca Indians in Ecuador. We heard about Amy Carmichael who opened an orphanage in India and Annie Armstrong the founder of the Women's Missionary Union. I found myself mesmerized by these stories and longed to do something as significant.

As the music played and the pastor waited, I felt a sense of tugging on my heart and soon found myself making my way down the aisle. When I got to the pastor he took my hand and I said, "I think God wants me to be a missionary." I'll never forget what happened next. This man of God patted me on the shoulder and said, "That's nice, dear." And then he had me sit on the pew in front.

I wasn't sure what was to happen next. Maybe I would go home and pack my suitcase and go to some faraway place, never to see my family again. But you can imagine my disappointment when nothing happened. The pastor never called me into his office to talk or encourage me. My parents never brought it up. Nothing.

I began to wonder. Had I made a mistake? Was I just imagining the tug on my heartstrings? I was just a kid, maybe God was only interested in adults. Finally, I put my dream of being a missionary on a shelf and forgot about it.

Our family was very involved in church, so it was natural for me to be active in many areas. After I married and had my own family, I continued my volunteer activities. I loved working in the church, serving the Lord, caring for His people. However, I never considered full time ministry.

Then one day the Women's Ministry Director at my church asked me if I would be willing to help her with some projects and programs she was working on. I was happy to help. We worked together for eight years. These were some of my most rewarding times in ministry. I loved working with the women at our church. I was learning a lot. It was during this time I began to study ministry and leadership.

In 1996 our Women's Ministry Director retired. Imagine my surprise when the Executive Pastor called me to his office and asked me to consider taking over the Women's Ministry at our church. "Who me?" I thought. After much prayer and consideration, I agreed to accept the position knowing I would have to depend on the Lord for a lot of help.

My first day on staff I took the elevator to the top floor of the Tower of Hope, the church administration building. This room had three walls of glass and served as a small chapel. This is where I often went to pray.

As I walked around the room looking at the view I had one of those "aha" moments. Our church was situated in the midst of Orange County, CA, a melting pot of cultures. To the north was a predominately Hispanic neighborhood, to the south and west was a large population of Asians, intermingled into these areas were pockets of African Americans and Caucasians. Rich and poor, educated and uneducated, men, women, and children who had not yet come to know the Lord.

I was brought back to that hot, humid day in the small church in Illinois when God tugged at my heart and asked me to be a missionary. Little did I know that this dream, would someday become a call and He would bring it to pass.

The definition of a missionary is one who is called and commissioned by the Lord to share the Gospel and make disciples, followers of Christ. God took the dream off the shelf that day. I knew then that I had not made a mistake. I had heard the Lord clearly, but I needed to allow Him time to groom me into the person He intended to use. Now I was ready, ready to make disciples.

If God has given you a dream, He will do the same thing for you. Trust Him. He has a plan.

> "'For I know the plans I have for you,' declares the LORD, 'plans to prosper you and not to harm you, plans to give you hope and a future'" (Jeremiah 29:11 NIV).

Gerry Wakeland is a speaker, writer and former women's ministry director. The mother of two daughters and grandmother of four boys, Wakeland currently resides in Albuquerque, New Mexico, while she pursues certification to become a spiritual director.

Acknowledgments

Thank you to each of the authors who contributed. Every story is the result of hard work and time and a commitment to sharing a message God has given them.

Thank you to Gerry Wakeland and CLASSEMINARS, INC. for the opportunity to learn through this journey and then produce a book to share with others.

Thank you to Bold Vision Books. Your work is always done with excellence.

Thank you to our Lord and Savior, Jesus Christ. Your love is reflected in each story. Speak to the heart of every reader through these words.

Made in the USA
Columbia, SC
04 October 2018